D1489099

Hints and Disguises

Hints and Disguises

Marianne Moore
and Her Contemporaries

By Celeste Goodridge

UNIVERSITY OF IOWA PRESS
IOWA CITY 🌵

University of Iowa Press, Iowa City 52242
Copyright © 1989 by the University of Iowa
All rights reserved
Printed in the United States of America
First edition, 1989

Typesetting by G&S Typesetters, Austin, Texas
Printing and binding by Thomson-Shore, Dexter, Michigan

Library of Congress Cataloging-in-Publication Data

Goodridge, Celeste.
    Hints and disguises: Marianne Moore and her contemporaries/by
Celeste Goodridge.—1st ed.
        p.   cm.
    Bibliography: p.
    Includes index.
    ISBN 0-87745-239-3
    1. Moore, Marianne, 1887–1972—Contemporaries.   2. Moore,
Marianne, 1887–1972—Knowledge—Literature.   3. American
poetry—20th century—History and criticism.   I. Title.
PS3525.O5616Z673   1989   89-4758
811′.52—dc19   CIP

For my mother and in memory of
Clare Elizabeth Barnett, 1954–1976

Contents

Acknowledgments

The late David Kalstone, who encouraged me to undertake this study as a dissertation, stands behind this book as a presence and voice who continues to influence and inspire my work. Elaine Showalter and Tom Edwards generously commented on this as a dissertation and provided essential advice concerning revisions for the book. The Graduate English Program of Rutgers University provided funds for some of my first trips to the Moore archive.

Sincere thanks to Pat Willis, the curator of American literature at the Beinecke Library of Yale University, for reading and discussing an earlier draft of the book and for sharing her extensive knowledge of Moore and the Moore archive with me; her guidance has been exemplary. Members of the Rosenbach Museum and Library staff, Ellen Dunlap, Evelyn Feldman, Leslie Morris, Carol Jones Neuman, and Joan Watson, have been most helpful during the course of my research. I am especially grateful to Marianne Craig Moore, Literary Executor for the Estate of Marianne Moore, for permitting me to cite unpublished material. Special thanks also to Peggy Fox, of New Directions, for clarifying issues of copyright law for me. Others have offered friendship and collegiality during the writing of this book. This cannot be acknowledged sufficiently, but thanks to Anne Blackford, Frank Burroughs, Brewster Buttfield, Helen Carson, Carol Colatrella, Charlotte Daniels, Anne Fleche, Carol McGuirk, Linda Kozusko, George and Cleo Kearns, Gayle Pemberton, Barry Qualls, Alan Nadel, Judy Novey, Mark Scott, Ed Shea, Johanna Smith, Linda Turzynski, William Watterson, and Jim Wood.

Grants from the Bowdoin College Faculty Development Fund made it possible for me to complete the research for this book. Several people have also helped bring the book to its closure. Robert Boenig typed the manuscript onto computer disks, making every step of the publishing process easier. Thanks to Gail Zlatnik of the University of Iowa for her meticulous copyediting of the manuscript.

My greatest debt is to Margaret M. Phelan for unwavering friendship, endless conversations, and for reading drafts of this with patience and freshness of perception; her observations and insights have been invaluable in shaping my own.

A Note
on the Text

All of Moore's final versions of the essays cited here can be found in *The Complete Prose* (1986). Since I am concerned with modernist reactions to these reviews and with the historical circumstances of their production, my citations refer readers to the texts of these essays as they originally appeared in the journals of the time.

Hints and Disguises

1 "Breasting the mode": Moore's Place in High Modernism

In connection with personality, it is a curiosity of literature how often what one says of another seems descriptive of one's self.[1]

On December 16, 1915, Marianne Moore wrote to her brother, John Warner Moore, that she would like to review some books for the *Philadelphia Ledger*:

> I should like to do books once a week for the magazine section and am doing a couple of sample reviews. I could tell them that I have followed the work of E.F.E. (in the Transcript) and J. B. Kerfoot in Life and Francis Hackett and Philip Littel in the N. Republic recently and what with my poems of a critical trend in the Egoist and Poetry & Others and C. Verse . . . I could certainly extort the position. I am prepared to review "poetry, fiction, art or theology." Music and sport and dancing are the only things I am afraid to tackle. I should write to them at once, but I am sure I could do more in an interview.[2]

With boldness and self-confidence, Moore confided to her brother that she imagined she could secure the position if given the opportunity to present herself in an interview. We see that her interest in writing criticism or reviewing books emerged at the same time that she started publishing her poetry; these two impulses were, as she implied to her brother, complementary. The act of reviewing was something she believed could be studied. With this in mind, Moore consciously chose models to follow: E.F.E., who wrote for the *Boston Evening Transcript*, J. B. Kerfoot, who wrote for *Life*, and Francis Hackett and Philip Littel, who both reviewed books for *The New Republic*. Although these popular and conventional writers do not in any respect predict the direction or shape her own reviews would take, it is significant that in 1915, the same year she published her first poems in *The Egoist* and in *Poetry*, Moore was attentively following some of the well-known reviewers of her time. She had even, as she told her brother, begun her apprenticeship by completing several sample reviews.

A year later, in 1916, Moore published her first critical statement, entitled "Samuel Butler," in *The Chimaera*.[3] Several months after that a longer and more developed critical essay of hers appeared in *The Egoist*. In "The Accented Syllable," she addresses fleetingly "tone of voice" in writers as different as Poe, Samuel Butler, Charles Hamilton Sorley, D. F. Dalston, and Wallace Stevens.[4] Later that same year Moore sent another short essay to *The Egoist*; in this piece, entitled "Poe, Byron, and Bacon," Moore took on the odd task of linking these three writers together.[5] Harriet Shaw Weaver, then the editor of *The Egoist*, wrote to her that although they did not intend to publish this, she hoped Moore would continue to send the magazine her critical essays.[6] H.D., who was then acting assistant editor, also encouraged Moore to send *The Egoist* her essays and reviews.

In 1918, Moore truly launched her career as a critic, reviewing Jean de Bosschère's poems, *The Closed Door*, T. S. Eliot's *Prufrock and Other Observations*, and William Butler Yeats' *The Wild Swans at Coole*. All three of these reviews appeared in *Poetry*. Her critical prose continued to appear through the sixties. In addition to the close attention she paid to the careers of the four most influential male modernist poets in America—Wallace Stevens, Ezra Pound, William Carlos Williams, and T. S. Eliot—Moore also reviewed Stewart Mitchell, Richard Aldington, Bryher, George Moore, H.D., Vachel Lindsay, E. A. Robinson, Maxwell Bodenheim, George Saintsbury, E. E. Cummings, Gertrude Stein, Alfred Kreymborg, Glenway Wescott, W. W. E. Ross, Conrad Aiken, Elizabeth Bishop, W. H. Auden, Louise Bogan, Kenneth Burke, and Babette Deutsch. This list, though by no means exhaustive, reveals the range of her critical interests.

Moore's role as a poet-critic, however, has not been fully assessed. The most obvious reason for this neglect is that until recently there were only two published collections of her prose: *Predilections* (1955) and *A Marianne Moore Reader* (1961). The critical reactions to *Predilections* have been mixed, but in no sense constitute a total evaluation of Moore's contribution to modernist discourse about poetry. Now that *The Complete Prose* (1986) is available, Moore's prose will probably begin to receive the critical attention her poetry has.[7]

Although there have been passing references to the intricacies of Moore's prose, most readers still think of her primarily as a poet. In his review of Moore's *Predilections*, Kenneth Burke praises the volume for being "a study in stylistic scruples,"[8] maintaining that Moore's "critical 'predilections' are the perfect analogue of her poetic 'observations.'"[9] Randall Jarrell calls *Predilections* "particular appreciation, not general criticism,"[10] contending that much of her prose is ultimately another version of her poetry. Laurence Stapleton asserts perceptively that Moore's "essays and reviews set up an imaginative discourse with the reader different from that maintained in her poetry,"[11] though, like Burke and Jarrell, she too is finally interested in Moore's prose as an important adjunct to her poetry. Although Bonnie Costello contends that "it is a mistake . . . to read these essays [in *Predilections*] primarily as appreciation, as Stapleton does,"[12] she limits her own discussion to Moore's "predilection for and strategy of indirection" in three representative essays: "Feeling and Precision," "Humility, Concentration and Gusto," and "Idiosyncrasy and Technique."[13] Donald Hall, the one critic who begins to take Moore's criticism on its own terms, seems to wish for an academic, expository tidiness in her criticism when he notes: "Her criticism is unsystematic, depending upon a juxtaposing of observations and quotations so that an overall impression emerges that could scarcely be called a thesis."[14]

We can speculate as to why Moore's prose has not been taken seriously by critics who have otherwise been committed to exploring her role as a poet. Moore herself may have contributed to her own neglect by giving her first collection of essays and reviews the seemingly equivocal title of *Predilections*. By allying her project with those of "impressionistic" critics, Moore relegated her readings to a lesser status in the eyes of those who by 1955 subscribed to Eliot's well-known distinction between the critic and the artist. In addition, her foreword to *Predilections*, which I discuss later, may have been perceived as self-effacing and thus have discouraged readers from giving her criticism the authority and autonomy they might have given that of Eliot, Pound, or Williams when their work was first collected.

Other critics have focused on Moore's role as editor of *The Dial* between 1925 and 1929 as a means of establishing her critical values.[15] Although one might be tempted to link what *The Dial* published while Moore was editor with her own critical values, this linkage is not smooth; for Moore's own daring, experimental, eccentric, yet catholic criticism stands in contrast to much of the criticism published during her tenure as editor. Between 1925 and 1929, for example, *The Dial* published John Eglinton, George Saintsbury, Bertrand Russell, George Santayana; and Logan Pearsall Smith. As editor of *The Dial*, Moore supported and did not try to change what was finally a conservative journal. In a letter to Saintsbury in 1926 Moore remarked, "Fortunately for The Dial I have only half power in decision, and often decline to use the whole of that."[16] Since Moore was, by her own admission, somewhat detached from the editorial decisions made at *The Dial*, it is dangerous to assume that *The Dial*'s values were her own.[17]

Now that *The Complete Prose* is available we can begin to evaluate Moore's role as a perceptive, often brilliant reader of her contemporaries; including nearly four hundred prose pieces written over the course of sixty years, the collection is an invaluable archive for scholars interested in Moore's *oeuvre*. Not all of it is of the same quality or interest. Throughout, however, we encounter a modernist sensibility of acute intelligence, unfailingly attentive to the culture of her time. Like the critical efforts of her contemporaries—Pound, Eliot, Williams, and Stevens—Moore's critical essays carve out an important version of the foundations of modernism.

Moore's essays and reviews allow us to reconstruct the public dialogues she had with the writers she valued most. Moore will be remembered both as a critic and as a prose stylist for her criticism of her contemporaries in the twenties, thirties, and forties. I focus on her criticism of Stevens, Pound, Williams, and Eliot because these were the poets against whom she most consistently measured her own poetics and practice. H.D. and Bishop might also be included, for they were also important to Moore; I have chosen not to include them because others have recently considered Moore's critical dialogues with them, particularly her private ones.[18] More important, although Moore reviewed their work when it initially appeared, she did not choose publicly to follow the trajectories of their careers over many years as she did those of the other four poets.

Moore's public and private critical exchanges with Stevens, Pound, Williams, and Eliot establish her centrality in this high modernist community; they also provide a new context for considering these poets' respective poetics and shifting alliances with one another. Moore's most compelling judgments of her contemporaries, as well as her own aesthetic, can best be recovered by examining the relationship between her private disclosures and her public pronouncements. Moore's archive, which she meticulously preserved, forces us to reassess the project of literary history and the legitimacy of the "private" document. My study posits that Moore's private writings—her letters, her reading and conversation notebooks, and her manuscript notes—are as valuable as her public offerings; it is only by reading these public and private documents in concert, and by recovering the dissonance or contradictions between them, that we can begin to evaluate Moore's contribution as a poet-critic and to sort out who she thought she was in this community and how the community perceived her.

Unlike other poet-critics such as Eliot and Pound, Moore dedicated herself almost exclusively to considering the achievements of her contemporaries.[19] In her review of *The Complete Prose*, Helen Vendler highlights this aspect of Moore's project: "It is easy to forget, in reading these hundreds of pieces with the security of hindsight, how much Moore was helping to make new works known, works not easy to absorb at first reading."[20] Although Stevens, Pound, Williams, and Eliot paid tribute to their peers (each of them at some point, for example, wrote about Moore), none of them followed any one of their contemporaries' careers over many decades as Moore did in her reviews. Between 1924 and 1964, for example, Moore reviewed almost every book of Stevens' poetry that appeared. She began by reviewing *Harmonium* in 1924 and ended in 1964 with a general tribute to Stevens' whole career that was published in *The New York Review of Books*.

As we conceive of canons today we tend to forget how much the public and private exchanges these writers had with one another about each other's work linked them in a common enterprise. Moore's correspondence with her contemporaries indicates how strong a sense of the importance of their collective critical mission she possessed. Her letters to Eliot, for example, reveal that for Moore, reviews, prefaces, and introductions launched the writer and text under consideration, becoming in the process part of the text itself. They offered the writer a protection of sorts from a public that would, at the very least, have to consider these public pronouncements before dismissing the book.[21]

Clearly Moore could never hope to give Eliot the kind of protection his two reviews of her work—his 1923 *Dial* review and his 1935 introduction to her *Selected Poems*—afforded her; and certainly, given his reputation after *The Waste Land* was published in 1922, Eliot did not in any real sense need launching. Moore did however believe that her reviews of Stevens, Pound, and Williams might counter the reactions of a potentially unreceptive public. Although she did not exclusively praise them,[22] she frequently chose to mask her reservations. Her recommendations of Stevens, Pound, and Williams are most interesting when they protect and praise and occasionally undermine or parody their enterprises. I am concerned with the aesthetic choices Moore made and the public alliances she cultivated when she disguised criticism that she might have offered openly.

Each of my chapters takes up in turn her method of approaching the careers of Stevens, Pound, Williams, and Eliot. With Stevens and Pound, Moore employs imitative appreciation—a strategy which allows her to offer her own stylistic translations of their temperaments. In her readings of Stevens, Moore imitates his "achieved remoteness," "his method of hints and disguises," and his "bravura"; in writing about Pound's project, she pays homage to his movement between "firm piloting" and "rebellious fluency."[23] Moore was deeply attracted to Stevens' and Pound's poetics, though in her treatments of their work she implicitly cautions against their respective tendencies to "'push certain experiments beyond the right curve of their art.'"[24] In her criticism of Pound, Moore also uses Eliot as someone against whom she could measure her own assumptions. Her references to Eliot in her copies of Pound's work and her extensive manuscript notes for her first review of the *Cantos* reveal how important Eliot's reviews of Pound were for shaping her own reading of him.

An analysis of the whole archive has been crucial in my study of her criticism of Williams. In my fourth chapter I document how Moore privately expressed reservations to Williams about his poetry, while in her published reviews of his work she usually disguised her ambivalence. In addition, Moore publicly used Stevens as a mask, reacting at times to his comments about Williams (comments that were not always favorable) rather than to Williams' work at hand. While she brings Eliot into her reviews of Pound, in her reviews of Williams Moore creates a critical alliance with Stevens that allows her to veil her increasing dissatisfaction with Williams' poetic and temperament. Moore distances herself from Williams and does not use imitative appreciation to approach his aesthetic as she does with Stevens and Pound; this may be seen as another indication of her dissatisfaction with his project.

Chapter 5 concerns Moore's differing perceptions of Eliot as a poet and as a critic. I discuss the way Moore enters the critical discourse surrounding his work in 1918 by setting up an imaginative, often stiff, relationship to a "reader" who may have misunderstood Eliot's work. The persona she creates allows her to hint at her own discomfort with Eliot's early poetry. When reviewing *The Sacred Wood* in 1921 for *The Dial*, Moore displays an unusual openness about publicly disagreeing with someone she was reviewing; this surfaces when she challenges Eliot's reading of Swinburne. In this review, Moore also offers a creative, though perhaps not intentional, misreading of Eliot's definition of criticism that allows her to praise the tendency of "impressionistic critics" to blur the distinction between criticism and creation. She was less open about aesthetic differences in her reviews of Eliot's poetry during the 1930s.

Moore makes her greatest contribution to modernist discourse about poetry when writing about these four poets. The critical exchanges Moore engaged in will prompt future readers to re-examine her own literary practice as well as that of her contemporaries. Perhaps the most important insight revealed by an examination of her private and public dialogues is that her deepest alliances were with Stevens and Pound, and not, as most have suggested, with Williams and Eliot. These preferences force us to reconsider the usual assumption that Moore and Williams, though temperamentally different, shared similar objectives in their poetic enterprises. Furthermore, Moore's readings of Stevens and Pound chart aesthetic links between their projects, thereby subverting the more traditional link between Pound and Eliot. Readers will thus return to Moore's own poetry with a new sense of the aesthetic confluence between her project and those of her high modernist contemporaries.

In a recent memoir for *Partisan Review*, Glenway Wescott, a lifelong friend of Moore's, delightfully captures her anomalous yet prominent position in "the literary establishment of the century":

Do you remember, can you see in memory, Rembrandt's so-called *The Night Watch*, which in fact is a day watch? It was left under a cover of darkened varnish for a long time, and this, added to the master's intentional chiaroscuro, misled even the art historians. About thirty upper-middle-class Amsterdam gentlemen constituting a guard of honor troop forward in most unmilitary order out of cavernous darkness into magical sunshine—all types: one almost royal looking, one haunted, perhaps by knowledge of a hopeless illness, and another corpulent and affluent; one with an angelic face, thrusting a lance all the way across the picture, as it were symbolically, and another who might be Don Quixote; a clown, a boor, a hobo, and a fanatic, and one conceivably a killer. In their midst, mystery of mysteries, a little childlike woman or womanly child, very blond, as in a dream, clad in numerous raiment of greenish gold; having, suspended from her belt, a white chicken with feet of gold; wearing also, on a ribbon, a rich purse or pouch.

Thus, to my imagination, Miss Moore had been, in the midst of her fellow writers, the literary establishment of the century. I often seem to myself deficient in humor, but when I first thought of this a while ago, I laughed aloud; and it amuses me still. If this were a lecture rather than an essay, and if I had a lantern slide of *The Night Watch* and a professorial pointer, perhaps I could attach twentieth-century literary names to all of Rembrandt's forgotten burghers . . . whether or not it made you laugh, you would easily perceive Miss Moore's likeness to the fairylike small personage who incomprehensibly strayed into Rembrandt's ken and captivated him while he was doing this vast commissioned work. . . . My point, worth thinking about, is that she was in the middle of the picture, a mystery in the middle of the picture—how did it happen?[25]

Wescott's highly stylized portrait of Moore appears at first glance to subscribe to some of the stereotypes associated with the "poetess."[26] Moore, a childlike figure who does not quite fit in, comes into this community of thirty upper-middle-class Amsterdam gentlemen presumably from the margin. Wescott may be alluding to Moore's own tendency—particularly late in her career—to present herself as an eccentric in a tricorne hat to a community that registered her eccentricities but also continued to value her presence. Striking a balance between this persona and her reception in this community, Wescott transforms her into a protective, almost magical presence who occupies the center of the painting while enjoying a certain anonymity. Even Rembrandt is portrayed as somewhat baffled by this creature who unexpectedly appears and captures his imagination. Wescott goes on to assert that with her contemporaries "she remained detached, full of her own devices." "Like the girl in Rembrandt's picture," he maintains, "her movement was crossways, from left to right, breasting the mode (mode after mode), traversing the parade, a law unto herself. . . ."[27]

Finally, Wescott forces us to revise the myth that Moore was someone who cultivated a detachment and reticence which kept her from contributing to and embracing the energies of this modernist community.[28] In his scheme, Moore acquires a prominence, a power, and a voice in this motley crew because of her mysterious position. "Armored" by her mobility—her ability to move in and out of this community at will—Moore enjoys the visibility of being in the center; yet she, unlike most of her contemporaries, is empowered by her anonymity—by being a mystery in this configuration.

This aspect of Moore's persona has led some critics to see her as someone who hid behind her "armor." Jarrell, for example, sees her poetic preoccupation with armored animals as indicative of her own need to be shielded.[29] Costello, on the other hand, writes energetically and perceptively about Moore's "images of sweetened combat"[30] in her poetry. For Costello, Moore's "imagery of armor is connected to a broader array of images of internalized combat, associated with the need for power and restraint in art, as in life."[31]

Although I do not examine images of armor or combat in Moore's prose, I view her strategies of self-concealment—her "hints and disguises"—as integral to her critical stance; Moore's economy of self-expenditure is contingent upon self-preservation. As she offers her critical assessments, we often have the sense that she holds something back. This strategy of withholding allows her to be, as Whitman is in "Song of Myself," both "in and out of the game." What I am suggesting is that Moore's self-presentation and her disclosures must be seen as inseparable from and even fueled by her concealment of self.[32] This self-presentation also characterizes Stevens' aesthetic and temperament; Stevens, as I point out in chapter 2, matched Moore in his strategies of evasion and in his insistence on maintaining his distance from others. Rather than seeing Moore's detachment and self-protectiveness as devices which kept her from expressing herself fully, I maintain that these self-imposed limits, which she carefully set up between herself and the world, were a necessary condition for her artistic expression.

Although Moore does not always praise her subjects, she often avoids publicly and overtly criticizing her contemporaries in her reviews of their work. It might be tempting to speculate, as some feminist critics have done, that Moore, as a woman poet-critic, could only enter the predominantly male critical discourse of her contemporaries in this muted fashion; this gender based assumption, however, is complex, given Moore's particular situation. Alicia Ostriker, in her discussion of Moore in *Stealing the Language: The Emergence of Women's Poetry in America*, presents one of the most compelling versions of this feminist thesis. Commenting on Moore's poetry, Ostriker contends that Moore's armor and camouflage "imply over and over the necessary timidities and disguises of a brilliant woman in a world where literary authority is male."[33] Seeing Moore's tendency to employ armor and armoring as symptoms of her discomfort with male literary authority, Ostriker maintains that the literary establishment perceived Moore as "the chaste and ladylike, self-effacing spinster in the tricorne."[34] Had she not been this way, Ostriker implies, Moore would not have gained acceptance in this community.

Such a reading reinforces, if only implicitly, the assumption that Moore wanted at any cost to be "one of the boys." It also serves to isolate Moore from virtually all of the other women writers of her time. Ostriker asserts:

> Yet would a sexual and powerful Marianne Moore have met with the respect accorded the chaste and ladylike, self-effacing spinster in the tricorne? There is no reason to think so. Amy Lowell's skill at self-promotion was defeated, of course, by the

larger skill of her enemy Ezra Pound amid jests of "Amygism" and jocular allusions to the poet's obesity and cigar smoking. Stein remained a figure of the coteries. Mina Loy, championed early by Pound and Eliot, scandalously famous in her time, fell silent and was forgotten. H.D., known as "the perfect imagiste" long after she had outgrown that diminutive label, continued to be represented in anthologies by her earliest and least disturbing poems, while her late work was dismissed as escapist by the few critics who noticed it. The aura of lesbianism about Lowell and Stein, of bisexuality about H.D., and of sexual cynicism about Loy, almost certainly inhibited their critical acceptability within the academy.[35]

Ostriker is interested in uncovering both Moore's subversive tendencies and the reasons critics have chosen to overlook them; however, she runs the risk of falsifying the full record by presenting Moore primarily in terms of the self-image Moore constructed later in her life.[36] When considering Moore's position as a poet-critic in the high modernist community in the twenties and thirties, a different persona emerges. As we examine her archive, particularly her unpublished correspondence with Stevens, Pound, Williams, and Eliot, we do not see someone who felt intimidated by male literary authority or excluded, as a woman, from this community.[37]

Moore's reluctance to become publicly embattled with Stevens, Pound, Williams, and Eliot, then, can most profitably be seen as an endorsement of a particular aesthetic, one that is in keeping with her belief that criticism and reviews, on one level, should protect the writer under consideration. For Moore, there is a grace and strength in withholding direct judgments—in making her reader strain to see what is deliberately always partially concealed. This critical stance is also, as I later demonstrate, an endorsement of an epistemology in which "things" are known by their parts—or through partial disclosure. Her temperament and her belief that art grows out of an economy of disclosure and concealment required that she value the unseen, the impenetrable, the inaccessible, the playful appearance of a sleight of hand, the mask or disguise, and the part, or partial view, over the whole. Moore takes a particular delight in simultaneously revealing and concealing the aesthetics of her contemporaries. As she masks and unmasks herself in her criticism of Stevens, Pound, Williams and Eliot, she attempts to achieve what she once said art aspires to: "a judicious balance between self-subordination and being one's self." [38]

Moore's public entry into the critical marketplace was circuitous and deserves examination. Moore's critics, for the most part, have considered her work in the context of her self-effacing presentation of herself and her art. Recently, however, her readers have begun to deconstruct this persona by documenting how deeply and consistently ambitious Moore was; they also claim she covered her tracks, often publicly and sometimes even privately, so that she would not appear to be so. [39] For example, as Margaret Phelan points out in her consideration of Moore's exchanges with H.D., Moore gave the retrospective impression to most people that she herself had nothing to do with the publication of her first book of poetry, while in fact, Phelan demonstrates, Moore began privately negotiating with H.D. about the volume as early as 1916. [40] Ostriker, who asserts that Moore's shyness "disguised an equally real arrogance," maintains that "her [1960] *Paris Review* interview is a self-presentation of the poet as self-deprecating literary virgin pulled reluctantly to the altar of publication." [41]

In keeping with her desire to conceal her ambition, Moore also avoided giving the appearance of directly and publicly promoting her critical enterprise. This reluctance may be seen in part as a way of compensating for her extraordinary ambition; it can also be seen as another version of her desire to vacillate between concealment and disclosure in her art. Her disguises took several forms. For example, she downplayed the scope of her endeavor by calling her critical pieces "reviews" instead of essays. Many of her "reviews," some of which were later revised for *Predilections*, surpassed in depth the reviews by other writers that appeared in the same little magazines. In a letter to George Saintsbury during her tenure as editor of *The Dial*, she indicated that she thought the essay more inherently revealing of its author:

> Every little while your essay on Poe is mentioned; Doctor Watson spoke of it especially when he was in the office a few days ago. . . . One reason that I have a leaning toward the essay form is that the presentment has somehow more of the identity of the writer than a review has.[42]

Thus by calling her own essays reviews, Moore took fewer overt risks and gave up less of her identity as a writer than if she had labelled her efforts essays. Reviews were publicly sanctioned to sell books and promote writers; they were a perfect medium for someone who wanted to enter the public arena but did not want a spotlight focused on her for attempting to move into this sphere.

Like many of her nineteenth-century predecessors, Moore also disguised her gender. In her 1918 review of Eliot's *Prufrock and Other Observations*, Moore refers to herself as "he" and as "this hardened reviewer"; both personae are of course misleading. While editor of *The Dial*, Moore also adopted for a brief time the pseudonym Peter Morris, disguising once again her gender and her identity.[43] While it might be tempting to read these aspects of Moore's self-presentation as indicative of her sensitivity to what Ostriker terms "male literary authority," we do well to note that there were many precedents among her male and female contemporaries for adopting pseudonyms which served to conceal both identity and gender. As Patricia C. Willis points out, Moore was following a convention at *The Dial* when she adopted a pseudonym:

Anonymous and pseudonymous contributions abounded in *The Dial*. All the short book reviews in the "Briefer Mention" section and most of the editors' "Comment" pages went unsigned. Repeatedly, Gilbert Seldes signed himself "Sebastian Cauliflower" and Dr. J. Sibley Watson, Jr. masked himself as "W.C. Blum," although both men wrote under their own names as well.[44]

Although Pound, Eliot, and Williams published collections of their prose as it accumulated, Moore did not publish a collection of her prose until 1955. There were several reasons for this delay. Moore's own reluctance to appear to be promoting herself openly was nothing new. It seems that Morton Zabel suggested, during his tenure at *Poetry* in the thirties, that Moore publish a collection of essays. In 1933 she wrote to H. S. Latham at Macmillan indicating that she often wrote reviews: "When not working on a piece of verse, I have written a book review or a notice of something that interested me, and it was suggested to me by Doctor Zabel of *Poetry* that I could sometime have a collection of essays published. However, I think essays are hard to market."[45] By stressing the general difficulty of marketing essays, Moore avoids the more important issue of how the public might react to a book of essays by her. She also balances her self-promotion with a certain amount of self-protection.

In 1944, however, she did send a collection of her prose to Macmillan. The Cummington Press had offered to publish a collection of it and since Macmillan was her publisher, she offered them the option first. In October of 1944 she wrote to W. H. Auden, describing Macmillan's unfavorable reaction to this option:

Regarding my turned down material, last spring the Cummington Press offered to publish certain prose of mine— reviews of Wallace Stevens, E. E. Cummings, Gertrude Stein, T. S. Eliot, my review of THE DOUBLE MAN, and one or two other papers. Macmillans have priority in publishing work of mine and since they asked to see the prose, I submitted it, suggesting that it perhaps be issued together with this present verse of mine which the company was about to publish. The prose was returned as not being a judicious companion piece for the verse; but also, I suspect, as not being of crucial interest.[46]

When *Predilections* was finally published in 1955 by Viking Press, Moore's publisher by this time, Moore disguised the range of her enterprise with the somewhat self-deprecating title. This proved—like her preference for calling her essays "reviews" or "papers"—to be still another device that may have served to discourage scrutiny of this collection and her work as a whole.

Her title of this first collection of prose (*Predilections*) as well as her foreword to it call attention to Moore's reluctance to give her judgments the immediate appearance of public authority that Eliot's or Pound's had from the start. Eliot's *Sacred Wood* certainly contained his "predilections," but he clothed them with a tone of authority that Moore's own would never have. The tone of Moore's foreword is noticeably self-effacing; it provides a strange and misleading frame for the "Predilections" that she presents:

Silence is more eloquent than speech—a truism; but sometimes something that someone has written excites one's admiration and one is tempted to write about it; if it is in a language other than one's own, perhaps to translate it—or try to; one feels that what holds one's attention might hold the attention of others. That is to say, there is a language of sensibility of which words can be the portrait—a magnetism, an ardor, a refusal to be false, to which the following pages attempt to testify.[47]

Echoing Eliot's description of the "impressionistic" critic in *The Sacred Wood*, Moore implicitly allies herself with critics such as Swinburne, Pater, and Symons.[48] Yet she, unlike her predeces-

sors, argues for the primacy of herself as a reader or translator in
an impersonal mode.

Moore's tone is detached, vague, and tentative: we see this
in her repeated use of "one" as well as in her reference to a
text as "something that someone has written." We encounter a
hesitance, caution, and reserve in the phrases "perhaps to trans-
late it," "try to," "might hold," and "attempt to testify." Yet this
foreword is a false advertisement for what actually follows.
Moore's guarded impersonal discourse posits a division between
herself as translator and the text or body of work she translates.
Frequently, however, her criticism engages in a breakdown of this
assumed division or hierarchy, elevating the "translation" or new
text over the one she is examining.

It is precisely this separation between the critic's discourse
about the text and the text itself that Eliot would argue must be
maintained and that "impressionistic" critics such as Pater and
Symons abandon. A brief examination of Moore's departure from
Eliot's view of the functions of both the critic and criticism will
illuminate the kind of bridge she forms between "impressionistic"
critics and contemporary critics.[49]

In 1923 in "The Function of Criticism" Eliot argues for a divi-
sion between criticism and creation:

> If so large a part of creation is really criticism, is not a large
> part of what is called 'critical writing' really creative? If so, is
> there not creative criticism in the ordinary sense? The answer
> seems to be, that there is no equation. I have assumed as axio-
> matic that a creation, a work of art, is autotelic; and that criti-
> cism, by definition, is *about* something other than itself.[50]

In *Criticism in the Wilderness*, Geoffrey Hartman maintains that
Eliot took this position to deny, as Matthew Arnold had earlier,
"that criticism can find its own justification, and be creative or
independent."[51] Moore, in contrast to Eliot, believes that criticism
can be "creative," thereby becoming "an autotelic activity." In

breaking down the assumed division between the text she exam-
ines and her own commentary, Moore anticipates contemporary
critics, who, according to Hartman, force us to ask: "What are
the proper relations between the 'critical' and 'creative' activities,
or between 'primary' and 'secondary' texts?"[52]

When H.D. wrote to Moore about Moore's review of her *Col-
lected Poems*, which appeared in *The Dial* in 1925, she implicitly
alluded to Moore's tendency to blur this distinction between pri-
mary and secondary texts:

> O my dear Marianne, what a beautiful review. I have not
> dared read it yet but glancing through, I came across my own
> prose quotation enshrined in your exquisite prose. What a
> more than doubly distilled subtlety. I stand glowing from the
> reflected splendour of Marianne and Sappho.[53]

Moore commits a creative theft as she appropriates and en-
shrines H.D.'s quotation/translation from Sappho in her own
prose commentary. In this moment Moore both pays tribute to
H.D.'s use of Sappho and creates a new context for H.D.'s quota-
tion, when she gives it a new setting in her own prose. When
H.D. calls Moore's text "a more than doubly distilled subtlety"
she acknowledges that Moore's commentary—her own distilla-
tion—is not subordinate to the text she quotes.

(Hartman raises similar issues about the function of critical
commentary in a more expository fashion. Although he main-
tains that "the critic is always a survivor or someone who comes
late,"[54] he also contends that "literary commentary may cross the
line and become as demanding as literature: it is an unpredictable
or unstable genre that cannot be subordinated, *a priori*, to its ref-
erential or commentating function."[55])

Moore's imitative appreciation of Stevens and Pound, the two
poets she valued most, also collapses the distinction between
commentary and text. As she imitates in her own prose style
some quality of their respective temperaments, or some stylistic

quality of theirs that she admires, Moore both pays homage to
their respective aesthetics and competes with them. That she
views imitation as an inherent mode of protection can be seen in
a comment she made about Elizabeth Bishop:

> One notices the deferences and vigilances in Miss Bishop's
> writing, and the debt to Donne and to Gerard Hopkins. We
> look at imitation askance; but like the shell which the hermit-
> crab selects for itself, it has value—the avowed humility, and
> the protection. Miss Bishop's ungrudged self-expenditure
> should also be noticed. . . .[56]

Imitation appears to appeal to Moore's own need to be self-
consciously generous in her self-expenditure and yet simultane-
ously hidden from view. In her criticism of Stevens and Pound,
we are exposed to a sensibility that thrives on the "verbal phys-
ics"[57] of revealing and concealing the self. Her method of ap-
proaching Stevens and Pound allows her to enter their worlds
and to remain simultaneously in a world of her own. Moore can
praise and compete with them, distancing herself in the process
from a public critical arena that emphasizes critical judgments
and reading instructions that lead to what Eliot called "the eluci-
dation of works of art and the correction of taste."[58]

Moore's reluctance to become publicly embattled, as well as
her role as "translator" of the difficult moderns, makes her the
heir to the critical enterprise of "impressionistic" critics such as
Swinburne, Pater, Wilde, and Symons. In *The Sacred Wood*, Eliot
describes Symons' criticism with its emphasis on "the faithful
record of the impressions":

> Mr. Symons, the critical successor of Pater, and partly of Swin-
> burne . . . *is* the "impressionistic critic." He, if anyone, would
> be said to expose a sensitive and cultivated mind—cultivated,
> that is, by the accumulation of a considerable variety of impres-
> sions from all the arts and several languages—before an "ob-

ject"; and his criticism, if anyone's, would be said to exhibit to us, like the plate, the faithful record of the impressions, more numerous or more refined than our own, upon a mind more sensitive than our own. A record, we observe, which is also an interpretation, a translation; for it must itself impose impressions upon us, and these impressions are as much created as transmitted by the criticism.[59]

In 1873 Pater had maintained: "What is important, then, is not that the critic should possess a correct abstract definition of beauty for the intellect, but a certain kind of temperament, the power of being deeply moved by the presence of beautiful objects."[60] Wilde also elevated the temperament of the critic over the object of scrutiny: "The highest criticism is the record of one's own soul."[61] Eliot disapproves of "impressionistic criticism" because it emphasizes the reader's, or critic's temperament and the reading process and does not assume that it is possible or desirable to see the work of art as autonomous.

The moment you try to put the impressions into words, you either begin to analyse and construct, . . . or you begin to create something else. . . . You may say this is not the criticism of a critic, that it is emotional, not intellectual—though of this there are two opinions, but it is in the direction of analysis and construction, . . . and not in the direction of creation. . . . The disturbance in Mr. Symons is almost, but not quite, to the point of creating; the reading sometimes fecundates his emotions to produce something new which is not criticism, but is not the expulsion, the ejection, the birth of creativeness.[62]

Although Eliot contends that all criticism begins with one's impressions, he differentiates between criticism that moves toward analysis and criticism such as Symons' that moves away from the construction of a system toward a mode of discourse which is neither criticism nor art, but hovers somewhere between the two.[63] For Eliot, the autonomous object of art may be lost in these moments.

Moore does not share Eliot's reservations. When writing about Stevens, Pound, Williams, and Eliot, she is interested in the aesthetic or sensibility behind the text rather than the text itself. Moore wants to recover or translate the temperament that makes Stevens' *Harmonium*, Pound's *Draft of XXX Cantos*, Williams' *Kora in Hell*, or Eliot's *Sacred Wood* possible. Her pageantry of responses to a writer and his text or texts is offered simultaneously as a translation and as a critique of the writer's aesthetic.

The conception that a text is autonomous is foreign to Moore. For her, texts are extensions of their authors that need to be translated—that come into being as they are read. Most criticism emphasizes the reader and the reading process; what is different in this instance is that Moore encounters an unstable form which achieves a momentary stability—a new shape—as she translates it. In contrast, Eliot and his New Critic followers, with their emphasis on the work of art, assume that the text is stable, recognizing the instability and tenuousness of all readings.

Moore often de-stabilizes the notion of what a text is. We see this particularly in her use of quotations. Her mosaic of quotations—from the text she is considering, the writer's other work, the writer on his own work, other writers on this writer's work, and any number of other subjects—creates a new text, one that competes with the "original." Kenneth Burke, who calls Moore's "pages" "a kind of critic's Mardi Gras" in which "the page becomes wholly an act of collaboration,"[64] also maintains that "when she quotes in her special way of quoting, we see her carving a text out of a text, much like carving a personal life out of life in general."[65]

Moore was fascinated by the use of quotation in poetry, criticism, and sermons and often marked passages in books or newspapers that discussed this technique. She marked, for example, a passage in George Saintsbury in which he notes that "the extraction and stringing together of quotations is far more troublesome than original writing."[66] She also marked a passage in Eliot's "Lancelot Andrewes" in which Eliot quotes Canon Brightman on Andrewes' use of quotations in his sermons: " 'His quotation is not decoration or irrelevance, but the matter in which he expresses what he wants to say.' "[67] Also, in a newspaper article that she clipped and saved, "In Mr. Pope's Grotto" by Victor Howes, Moore made a mark in the margin beside the following passage:

> Nor is that all that can be said on the grotto's behalf. For the process of making a grotto and the process of making a poem were curiously alike with Pope. Both the grotto and the poems are models of the lapidary art, the art of assembling with patience and care a vast number of small units from a wide variety of sources, and then of arranging them so that they fuse into a meaningful and harmonious whole.[68]

Moore, we can infer from both her criticism and her poetry, is also interested in the setting created for these units, or fragments, which are gathered from a variety of different places.

She was also influenced in her use of quotation by seventeenth-century writers such as Bacon, Browne, and Burton, her formal knowledge of whom dates from an English course she took in "Imitative Writing" in 1909 while studying at Bryn Mawr College.[69] A writer like Burton, for example, frequently calls our attention to the process of making a text. In the following passage from *The Anatomy of Melancholy*, we hear a person—one whom Moore would both understand and sympathize with—who vacillates between protecting and exposing himself and between consciously shaping his text out of other texts and distancing himself from this process.

> As a good housewife out of divers fleeces weaves one piece of cloth, a bee gathers wax and honey out of many flowers, and makes a new bundle of all, *Floriferis ut apes in saltibus*

omnia libant [as bees in flowery glades sip from each cup], I have laboriously collected this cento out of divers writers, and that sine injuria, I have wronged no authors, but given every man his own. . . . I cite and quote mine authors (which, howsoever some illiterate scribblers account pedantical, as a cloak of ignorance, and opposite to their affected fine style, I must and will use). . . . The matter is theirs most part, and yet mine, apparet unde sumptum sit [it is plain whence it was taken] (which Seneca approves), aliud tamen quam unde sumptum sit apparet, [yet it becomes something different in its new setting]. . . . I do concoquere quod hausi [assimilate what I have swallowed], dispose of what I take. . . . the method only is mine own. . . .[70]

Burton's Renaissance habit of mind is in keeping with Moore's own temperament. The meditation that we overhear is about creating a distinct voice and about protecting the identity of that voice. Burton courts a dependence on these different writers only to assert his independence from them. He playfully and perhaps self-deprecatingly refers to himself as a "good housewife" who "out of divers fleeces weaves one piece of cloth," but, he reminds us, his collection acquires a new identity as he creates a new setting for it.

Like Burton and other seventeenth-century writers, Moore uses quotations to give her voice a certain authority as well as a certain protection. Like Burton, Moore can both promote and conceal herself. Her quotations, like his, contribute to our sense of someone "writing to the moment"—composing as she proceeds. They also serve to interrupt this process; her quotations can disrupt the pace of her sentences, contributing at times to the appearance of an explosion within them. Laurence Stapleton points out that "quotation may build an otherwise unobtainable extension of experience from one activity of life to another,"[71] but what has not been noticed is the extent to which Moore relies on quotation in her criticism as a mask or a way of momentarily distancing herself from the issue at hand.

Moore's aesthetic preference for the part over the whole also explains in part why quotation is so important to her. "Only as one isolates portions of the work," Moore writes in her 1923 review of H.D.'s *Hymen*, "does one perceive the magic and compressed energy of the author's imagination. . . ."[72] As Moore translates her contemporaries, she tends to weave portions of their work into her own sentences; Moore's discourse operates at the level of the sentence and sometimes even at the level of the phrase, thus my readings focus on her sentences.

Like Joyce, whose image of the gnomon defines the aesthetic operating in *Dubliners*, Moore asks us to take the fragment as representative of the whole. William Carlos Williams' 1925 assessment of her poetry provides a frame for this aesthetic preference. Williams argues that Moore's poetry simultaneously creates and destroys poetic forms. Likening this paradoxical aesthetic to focusing on a crack in a bowl, Williams creates a metaphor for Moore's project which, like Joyce's gnomon, reminds us that for the modernist, all knowledge is incomplete and fragmented:

> If one come with Miss Moore's work to some wary friend and say, "Everything is worthless but the best and this is the best," adding, "—only with difficulty discerned," will he see anything, if he be at all well read, but destruction? From my experience he will be shocked and bewildered. He will perceive absolutely nothing except that his whole preconceived scheme of values has been ruined. And this is exactly what he should see, a break *through* all preconceptions of poetic form and mood and pace, a flaw, a crack in the bowl. It is this that one means when he says destruction and creation are simultaneous.[73]

For Williams, Moore's poetic form achieves a permanence when it is most unstable, fragmented, and fragile. Moore does not shy away from the flaw; rather, she invites us to see the crack in the bowl as inseparable from the perception of the bowl itself.

The pages that follow attempt to define the implications of this aesthetic as it takes shape in Moore's prose, specifically in her criticism of her contemporaries Stevens, Pound, Williams, and Eliot. When possible I explore aesthetic differences between Moore and her contemporaries, especially those which emerge in her private exchanges with them but are silenced, or only hinted at, in her public reviews of their work.

2 "Aristocratic cipher": Moore's Reviews of Stevens

> . . . power is tolerable only on condition that it mask a substantial part of itself. Its success is proportional to its ability to hide its own mechanisms.[1]

> Thanks for the copy of Miss Moore's review [of *Ideas of Order*]. She is one of the angels: her style is an angelic style. It is just as unique as Gertrude Stein's and, to my way of thinking, makes Miss Stein seem shallow.[2]

Although Moore and Wallace Stevens did not meet until 1943, they corresponded over the years; during the twenties, when Moore was editor of *The Dial*, she solicited poetry and prose from him. Her 1924 review of *Harmonium*, which appeared in *The Dial*, was by all accounts one of the most perceptive and favorable reviews Stevens received. In the thirties, she reviewed Stevens' *Ideas of Order* (1936) and *Owl's Clover* (1937); in 1935, Stevens published his first essay about her work. These public and private exchanges continued throughout the forties and fifties; in 1953, for example, Stevens suggested to Herbert Weinstock, his editor at Knopf, that Moore choose the poems for the proposed Faber and Faber edition of his *Selected Poems*.[3]

While their private exchanges over the years were increasingly warm, publicly Moore continued to maintain a certain distance. We see this when she describes their first meeting. "I first met

Wallace Stevens in 1943," Moore writes in 1964, "at Mount Holyoke where my mother and I were attending the Entretien de Pontigny, presided over by Professor Gustave Cohen, the mediaevalist."[4] She focuses on Stevens' presence: "Mr. Stevens—sitting at a table under a tree—gave a lecture, 'The Figure of the Youth as a Virile Poet' (included later in *The Necessary Angel*) about imagination, and spoke of Coleridge dancing on the deck of a Hamburg packet, dressed all in black, in large shoes and worsted stockings."[5] (In *Parts of a World: Wallace Stevens Remembered*, Peter Brazeau also refers to the occasion: "At 10:30 A.M. that balmy Wednesday, [Stevens] settled into one of the chairs that had been set up under the large elms near Porter Hall and began to read his paper . . . to the men and women gathered on the lawn."[6] Brazeau also points out that "Stevens' usual distance from his audience affected the proceeding itself."[7] Moore, who was a participant in the conference, was actually sitting next to Stevens and thus facing the audience herself; she gives the impression, however, that like everyone else her "meeting" with Stevens involved watching, absorbing, and admiring his performance from afar.[8])

Although Moore's anecdote appears in her last critical piece on Stevens—a retrospective essay written for *The New York Review of Books* in 1964—it expresses a familiar paradigm in their literary relationship. For some time Moore had conceived of Stevens as the quintessential maestro in her poetic sphere, as the greatest poet of her generation. He was, as she asserted in her 1937 review of *Owl's Clover*, "America's chief conjuror—as bold a virtuoso and one with as cunning a rhetoric as we have produced."[9] For Moore, Stevens' performance depends upon his trickery; he achieves his effect by secret means. Thus, throughout her reviews of Stevens, Moore conveys the extent to which he always seems to hold something back from us: like a magician whose performance at its best conceals the effort that went into it.

Moore clearly seems to have attributed some of Stevens' success to his ability "to live in an unspoiled cosmos of his own. . . . "[10]

She connected his evasiveness to his desire to make a world of his own, apart from this one. Yet as she maintained in her 1924 *Dial* review of *Harmonium*, Stevens' efforts to escape were not always easy: "In his book, he calls imagination 'the will of things,' 'the magnificent cause of being,' and demonstrates how imagination may evade 'the world without imagination'; effecting an escape which, in certain manifestations of *bravura*, is uneasy rather than bold." [11] Perhaps recognizing something of her own temperament in Stevens, Moore was Stevens' first reader to imply that his extravagant gestures of escaping grew out of a discomfort with the world he inhabited.

Moore championed Stevens over many decades, recognizing most perceptively that his aesthetic, like her own, depended upon both his "achieved remoteness" and his "method of hints and disguises." [12] And, although in her reviews she expressed an occasional uneasiness about Stevens' tendency to take these gestures too far, usually she partially disguised this suspicion. When writing about William Carlos Williams' work, Moore also chose to mask her reservations, though privately she insisted on expressing her increasing discomfort with his enterprise. My readings, in both cases, seek to recover the muted reservations because they invariably illuminate Moore's own poetic.

Although Moore first wrote publicly about Stevens in 1924, when she reviewed *Harmonium* for *The Dial*, she began thinking of writing something about him as early as 1916. On November 10, 1916, she wrote to H.D., then an assistant editor of *The Egoist*, expressing her interest in Stevens:

I should like to try a comparison of George Moore and Fielding; also one of Knut Hamsun and Carlyle and one of Wallace Stevens and Compton Mackenzie. I am very much interested also, in William Williams' work, but I am a little afraid to undertake a criticism of it. I feel that I have not seen enough of it to justify my writing one. [13]

By 1916 Moore had most likely seen Stevens' poems in *Poetry* (1914) and *Others* (1915).[14] This early familiarity with his work accounts for the comprehensive nature of her first review, which appeared eight years later.[15]

Moore's interest in Stevens' career spanned six decades, if we include the decade in which she began reading his poetry. Between 1924 and 1964 she published eleven pieces of criticism about him.[16] Although Moore reviewed individual collections of his poetry (usually when they appeared), she committed herself to an exploration of his *oeuvre* and the consistency of his canon. This concern places Moore at the beginning of the ongoing critical debate over whether there is an aesthetic consistency between Stevens' early poems and his later ones.

In 1936 when Moore wrote to Stevens to tell him that *The Criterion* had accepted her review of *Ideas of Order*, she stressed the "enviable unity" of the volume:

> T. S. Eliot wrote me of being delighted to be able to include in *The Criterion* a review of you. I recall hearing, through a protracted dinner, no topic discussed but your verse, and am sceptical of your not being surfeited and impeded with initiate compliments of the delicate sort. *Ideas of Order* is an enviable unity—a kind of volume-progression on certain individual poems of previous years, and were it not that one feels a fool in saying what is no secret, it would be a temptation to particularize.[17]

After her 1924 review of *Harmonium*, Moore addresses the unity of his work as a whole; she treats the arrival of new poems in terms of their connection to his earlier poems. While preparing her review of *Owl's Clover*, Moore made the following note: "*Owl's C int.* especially as it fits into the other work."[18] In 1940 she praised Stevens for "the interacting veins of life between his early and later poems. . . ."[19] And in 1943, she began her review of Stevens' *Parts of a World* and *Notes Toward a Supreme Fiction* by asserting "it is a happy circumstance that we have *Notes Toward a Supreme Fiction* not long after *Parts of a World*, for they are inseparably interrelated roots of the same tree."[20] Read as a group in which the parts illuminate the whole, Moore's reviews of Stevens build on one another. Her concerns include the power of the imagination, Stevens' use of color and light, his ability to create "several languages within a single language,"[21] and, most important, his masks and disguises.

In a letter to Ronald Lane Latimer on August 13, 1935, Stevens wrote that "selling poetry now-a-days must be very much like selling lemonade to a crowd of drunks."[22] In saying this, Stevens acknowledged the hostility of the general public to the modernist enterprise; he also called attention to the difficulties most of them had trying to sell, promote, and obtain visibility for their poetry in an unreceptive marketplace.

Moore's answer to this ongoing dilemma was to "translate" the moderns and defend their need to be difficult. On October 4, 1935, she wrote to T. S. Eliot at *The Criterion* about her review of Stevens' *Ideas of Order*; in this letter she conveys both her concern with publishing her review of Stevens and with giving his book visibility:

> It is a pleasure to me that you expect to use my review of Wallace Stevens. He seems to read what you write yourself and it naturally will gratify him that you think his book matter for review; and for my own sake, it being hard for one to find homes for one's cats.[23]

Although Moore wishes to give Stevens some publicity, she also seems curiously protective of him and of her own role as promoter-reviewer. Often in her reviews of Stevens, Moore adopts a slightly antagonistic attitude toward his readers, seeing herself, at least in part, as a mediator or buffer between his work and the public that receives it. Praising Stevens for his distance from the philistines, Moore maintains in her 1936 review of *Ideas of Order* "the altitude of performance makes the wild boars of philistinism who rush about interfering with experts, negligible."[24] Later that year in a letter to Stevens, Moore thanks him for the copy of *Owl's Clover* he sent her. In this letter she suggests that Stevens' disguises allow him to maintain his distance. This time she seems to identify with his readers, whom she terms "the tenantry." Equating his success with his disguises and his distance from her, Moore joins "the tenantry" in her salute to Stevens, who stands with "still persisting members of an aristocracy":

> *Owl's Clover* received from you this morning, I had been reading, having been sent the pages by *Poetry*—I would not say for review, no review of such precipitates and beauties being possible—but for comment; and it made me hope for you that in giving to the world one gives to oneself. The world probably is not owl enough to thank you for troubling about it; but an unkilled and tough-lived fortitude is a great help to us, conveyed as it is by your disguises, and may I say as the tenantry say to still persisting members of an aristocracy, "long life to it," to this hero which you exemplify.[25]

Moore not only accepts but, more important, defends the necessity of Stevens' disguises. Contributing to the strength of his vision, they constitute an essential component of his aesthetic. In her 1937 review of *Owl's Clover*, Moore returns to this feature of Stevens' work:

> They [Stevens' poems] embody hope, which in being frustrated becomes fortitude; and they prove to us that the testament to emotion is not volubility. It is remarkable that a refusal to speak should result in such eloquence and that an implied heaven could be made so definite.[26]

As late as 1964, in her last critical essay about Stevens, Moore again defines him in terms of his distance from his public and notes his reluctance to cater to "bewildered readers."

> He was equipoise itself, although he could be displeased—in fact, angered by an imposter. People have a way of saying, "I don't understand poetry. What does this mean?" The query does not seem to me contemptible. However, Wallace Stevens did not digress to provide exegeses for bewildered readers.[27]

Despite her recognition that Stevens' art succeeds, in part because of what she described in 1924 as his "aristocratic cipher" and what in 1936 she called his "practised hand at . . . open cypher," Moore occasionally voices an uneasiness about Stevens' disregard for his readers, his reserve, his impenetrability, and his temperament.[28] "Willingness to baffle the crass reader," Moore asserts in her 1943 review of *Parts of a World* and *Notes Toward a Supreme Fiction*, "sometimes baffles the right one. That is to say, interrupted soliloquy can amount to disrupted logic."[29] In a letter to William Carlos Williams in 1944, Moore also confides:

> Wallace Stevens is beyond fathoming, he is so strange; it is as if he had a morbid secret he would rather perish than disclose and just as he tells it out in his sleep, he changes into an uncontradictable judiciary with a gown and a gavel and you are embarrassed to have heard anything. . . .
>
> His firm stanzas hang like hives in hell
> Or what hell was, since now both heaven and hell
> Are one, and here, O terra infidel.
> . . . .
>
> Whatever this is saying, it is impossible to gainsay. ? ?[30]

In this private admission to Williams, Moore almost becomes one of Stevens' puzzled and frustrated readers. Stevens is so difficult to pin down that even when he reveals some gloomy hidden secret, he still escapes our comprehension. His disclosure here, Moore implies, makes her uncomfortable. As he assumes the role of a judiciary, who cannot be opposed, Moore is embarrassed to have been privy to his confession. Despite her protest to Williams that she cannot comprehend what Stevens is saying in this stanza from the third section of his "Esthétique du Mal," Moore may in fact be embarrassed or troubled by what Stevens reveals about himself, or at least hints at, in this section of the poem. As Helen Vendler eloquently suggests, the poem is a "lyric examination of the evil most tempting for Stevens—the evil of nostalgia and self-pity, the appetite for sleek ensolacings—or worse, a 'scholarly' interest in his own pain."[31] Is Stevens' examination of self-pity the "morbid secret" Moore wished she had not overheard? Or is she perhaps offended by Stevens' flirtation with "an over-human god" who pities "us so much?" Moore was undoubtedly also disturbed by the blasphemous assertion that "now both heaven and hell / Are one. . . ." What seems to trouble her most, however, is that Stevens abandons his usual self-restraint in this poem; yet he remains protected, armored and empowered by his ability to be both the confessor and the judge of his confession. Finally, Moore concedes the power of Stevens' controlled disclosure when she asserts that while she is not sure what he is saying, she cannot resist or deny the authority of Stevens' expression.

Over the years in her reviews of Stevens Moore increasingly camouflaged her occasional discomfort with any aspect of Stevens' temperament. In her 1924 review of *Harmonium*, however, she displays an uncharacteristic willingness to confront Stevens' intentional boorishness:

> One resents the temper of certain of these poems. Mr. Stevens is never inadvertently crude; one is conscious, however, of a deliberate bearishness—a shadow of acrimonious, unprovoked contumely. Despite the sweet-Clementine-will-you-be-mine

nonchalance of the "Apostrophe to Vincentine," one feels one-self to be in danger of unearthing the ogre and in "Last Looks at the Lilacs," a pride in unserviceableness is suggested which makes it a microcosm of cannibalism.[32]

Moore suggests that in poems like "Apostrophe to Vincentine" and "Last Looks at the Lilacs," Stevens' speaker displays a certain gratuitous cruelty that cannot be overlooked; his various dis-guises and rhetorical strategies, she implies, do not excuse his be-havior in these poems. In short, Moore insinuates that Stevens adopts particular masks which he thinks give him the license to be cruel. Moore anticipates some of Stevens' best readers in pointing to this dissonance in his poetic.[33]

For Moore, the habit of mind she encounters in some of Ste-vens' early poems is connected to his aesthetic preference for re-maining aloof; her manuscript notes make it clear that she finds the pride which accompanies this posture unacceptable:

> W. Stevens—a pride in unserviceableness
>   that is not synon. with the beauty of
>   ness
>   aloof~~ness~~ self~~sufficiency~~
> ~~the fairy & the brute~~
>   a bg ogre stalking toward one w a knobbed
>   club . . .
> Stevens recoils from admitting the force of the
>   basic emotions.[34]

Given her own poetic, Moore recognizes the beauty and the power of Stevens' desire to remain aloof; when not associated with self-reliance and humility, however, the form it takes can be dangerous. Stevens exhibits a rudeness or surliness which, she maintains, allows him to retreat from confronting certain basic emotions. His detachment allows him to behave reprehensibly, without confronting the implications of his behavior.

Bonnie Costello points out that these manuscript notes appear in Moore's working notes for "The Plumet Basilisk" and that Moore's exotic imagery in this poem may be seen as a tribute to Stevens and his imagery in "The Comedian as the Letter C." Costello also draws a parallel between Stevens' alligator in "Nomad Exquisite" and Moore's basilisk.[35] Costello's reading, however, ignores the negative comments about Stevens' enterprise that we find in Moore's manuscript notes for both her review of *Harmonium* and her poem "The Plumet Basilisk." It seems to me that Moore's basilisk may be both a tribute to Stevens' temperament—a temperament that thrives on evasions and disguises—and a critique of Stevens' "quicksilver ferocity":

> he is alive there
>   in his basilisk cocoon beneath
> the one of living green; his quicksilver ferocity
>   quenched in the rustle of his fall into the sheath
> which is the shattering sudden splash that marks his temporary
>   loss.

Moore was fascinated and occasionally frustrated by Stevens' rapid retreats. Costello maintains that as Moore "remarks [in her reviews] on Stevens' swiftness and elusiveness, his 'incandescent' surfaces, his 'disguises,' we cannot help but think of her own writing as well."[36] A reading of the public and private exchanges of Moore and Stevens highlights the important similarities between their respective aesthetics; what has not been explored, however, is the extent to which Moore celebrates Stevens' need to cultivate his disguises even while sometimes protesting his inaccessibility. The tendency to praise and to undermine Stevens' poetic often emerges in Moore's reviews when she identifies Stevens' disguises, deceptions, and calculated distance. We see this, for example, in her 1924 review of *Harmonium* when she describes Stevens' "achieved remoteness":

One feels, however, an achieved remoteness as in Tuh Muh's lyric criticism: "Powerful is the painting . . . and high is it hung on the spotless wall in the lofty hall of your mansion." [37]

If the simile seems to unmask some quality of Stevens, the metaphor serves to reinstate his inaccessibility. Moore first compares Stevens' detachment to Tuh Muh's in his lyric criticism; then she implicitly likens his desired seclusion to an inaccessible painting that nevertheless retains its autonomy and well-defined place "on the spotless wall in the lofty hall." Like a Chinese box that opens only to reveal another box, Moore's masks multiply in deference to those of Stevens. As she embeds her quotation from "Tuh Muh's lyric criticism" into her sentence, Moore drops out of sight, concealing her own presence and the overt judgment that Stevens' retreats from his readers were sometimes taken too far.

In her 1936 review of *Ideas of Order* published in *The Criterion*, Moore also creates a range of masks behind which she sequesters both Stevens and herself:

> Wallace Stevens can be as serious as the starving-times of the first settlers, and he can be Daumier caricaturing the photographer, making a time exposure watch in hand, above the title, *Patience Is an Attribute of the Donkey.* [38]

Moore's comic list of analogies is excessive; we can hardly locate Stevens among the first settlers, Daumier, the photographer, and the photographer's title. Her analogy between Daumier and Stevens, however, is suggestive, for Daumier, like the poet, maintained a distance from the artistic circles of his time. By comparing Stevens to Daumier, Moore may also be suggesting that Stevens, like the caricaturist, insisted on distorting his subjects.

In this same review of *Ideas of Order*, Moore also compares Stevens to Brahms and his "technique of evasion":

> In the untrite transitions, the as if sentimental unsentimentality, the meditativeness not for appraisal, with hints taken from

the birds, as in Brahms, they recall Brahms; his dextrousness,
but also his self-relish and technique of evasion as in the inci-
dent of the lion-huntress who was inquiring for the celebrated
Herr Brahms: "You will find him yonder, on the other side of
the hill, this is his brother."[39]

In "Anglais Mort à Florence," Stevens' speaker refers to Brahms
as "his dark familiar" and "that dark companion." Moore un-
doubtedly draws on this association. Brahms, like Stevens, could
be reticent, evasive, and introverted; also, Brahms, like the poet
and Daumier, often chose not to frequent the artistic circles of his
contemporaries. Moore pays Stevens a high compliment by not-
ing that he is like Brahms in his tendency to reflect or meditate
on things; yet this encomium is partially belied by what follows.
In a comic vein, Moore describes the pleasure Brahms seems to
take in escaping from the lion huntress. The tone of this incident,
whether apocryphal or true, threatens to trivialize both Stevens'
evasions and our own desire as readers to pin him down. Moore's
use of an anecdote from Brahms' biography, complete with a
quotation, is a way of distancing herself—a way of imitating in
her own style Stevens' own need to elude his readers. Moore's
apparent neutrality here allows her to avoid passing a public
judgment on Stevens' or Brahms' ability to evade us.

In her 1937 review of *Owl's Clover*, however, she makes Stevens
into a benign transgressor when she compares his behavior to
Mercury's.

His method of hints and disguises should have Mercury as their
patron divinity, for in the guise of "a dark rabbi," an ogre, a
traveller, a comedian, an old woman, he deceives us as the god
misled the aged couple in the myth.[40]

Stevens' different guises in poems such as "Le Monocle de Mon
Oncle" ("a dark rabbi"), "Floral Decorations for Bananas" ("an

ogre"), and "The Comedian as the Letter C" ("a traveller" and "a comedian") are compared to Mercury's different postures. Mercury is known for his cunning. Like the Stevens Moore describes in her 1944 letter to Williams, Mercury moves easily between two worlds and is never punished for this.[41] In Book Eight of Ovid's *Metamorphoses*, Baucis and Philemon (Moore's "aged couple in the myth") entertain Jove and his mischievous son Mercury, who have come to earth in disguise in order to test the piety and generosity of those they meet. Many wealthy homes turn them away, but Baucis and Philemon, who are poor, receive Jove and Mercury with great hospitality. As a result, the gods reveal their identity, save the couple from a flood, and later, when Baucis and Philemon request to die at the same time, turn them into trees whose boughs intertwine. Moore may be implying that Stevens, like Mercury, tests his readers with his "hints and disguises."

As late as 1952 Moore points to one of the advantages of Stevens' disguises. "Wallace Stevens," she contends, "embeds his secrets, inventing disguises which assure him freedom to speak out. . . . "[42] At this point in his career, Moore felt that Stevens' disguises and secrets were empowering, that they allowed him a certain freedom to express himself. In her earlier reviews, particularly her 1924 review of *Harmonium*, Moore believed that Stevens' aesthetic depended upon his masks, but she did not always embrace them. Nevertheless, Moore recognized in a way that none of Stevens' early critics did that his poetic depended upon the dissonance between his disguises and his disclosures.

Throughout her reviews, Moore is usually not interested in revealing the secrets Stevens so carefully embeds in his work; she is more committed to pointing to qualities of his aesthetic or temperament that are baffling or incomprehensible. We see this in her review of *Harmonium*, when she criticizes Stevens for his inability to be decisive:

There is a certain bellicose sensitiveness in

> "I do not know which to prefer . . .
> The blackbird whistling
> Or just after,"[43]

Moore expresses her discomfort with the tone of these lines from "Thirteen Ways of Looking at a Blackbird." She conceals this reservation from immediate recognition by using the strategy of imitative appreciation—a strategy that has consistently been associated with praise. The phrase "bellicose sensitiveness" imitates Stevens' indecision about "which to prefer"—the sound itself or the memory of it. But Moore's imitation is not wholly laudatory; her oxymoron captures Stevens' habitual hesitation to commit himself to a particular position and exposes the potentially belligerent or combative energy of his "sensitiveness."

In her 1937 review of *Owl's Clover*, in which she defends Stevens for being difficult, for doing that which may contribute to ambiguity or vagueness, Moore highlights Stevens' achievement and mocks it:

> We are able here, to see the salutary effect of insisting that a piece of writing please the writer himself before it pleases anyone else; and how a poet may be a wall of incorruptibleness against any concessive violating of the essential aura of contributory vagueness.[44]

In an effort to placate the reader who complains about Stevens' inaccessible manner and wants to alter his technique, Moore parodies the language of a legal document that promises some exchange of information. But Moore's own opacity here—her own impenetrable vagueness—may be more than just a tribute to, and a defense of, Stevens. Her style of approaching his work simultaneously protects Stevens and disguises her own possible ambivalence from immediate detection. As she reveals some quality of his aesthetic only to mystify it, Moore's method of ap-

proaching Stevens mirrors and competes with Stevens' own per-
formance of disclosure and concealment.

In deference to the baroque energies of Stevens' poetry, Moore
frequently mimes these energies in her own style. Drawing on the
use of exploded periods, similes that defy their own implicit limits
by blossoming into metaphor, elaborate visual conceits, antithe-
ses, classical allusions, an extravagant fusion of various discourses
such as those of poetry, music, dance, and sports, and quotations
that disrupt the pace of her sentences, Moore enacts in her own
style the epistemological implications of Stevens' vision. As her
sentences unfold, often upsetting the expectations they have set
up, Moore mirrors in her own style Stevens' preference for "a
permanence composed of impermanence,"[45] "the solid, but the
movable, the moment,"[46] and the approach to the subject over
the subject itself. While Moore's imitative appreciation recreates
or translates for us the aesthetic behind Stevens' work, it also
provides a commentary on the aesthetic consanguinity between
her work and Stevens'.

In her homage to Stevens' imagination in her 1924 review of
Harmonium, Moore creates a strikingly visual baroque conceit for
the imagination that rivals Stevens' own tendency to move in
seemingly contradictory directions:

> Imagination implies energy and imagination of the finest
> type involves an energy which results in order "as the motion
> of a snake's body goes through all parts at once, and its volition
> acts at the same instant in coils that go contrary ways."[47]

The structure of the sentence mirrors the snake's motion. The
contrary energy of the sentence imitates the coils of the snake.
In the first part of the sentence we experience a mind tentatively
groping after knowledge and defining, with increasing preci-
sion, the terms of that knowledge: "Imagination implies energy /
and imagination of the finest type involves an energy / which re-
sults in order. . . ." These divisions suggest that we read the sen-

tence up to this point in increments; no part of the sentence is
subordinate to the whole. After the clause—"which results in or-
der"—we expect closure or a more prolonged pause, and yet just
as Moore creates this resting place, she shifts her energies to what
appears to be a simile introduced by "as" but what is in fact an
elaborate metaphor. Her embedded quotation here breaks the
sense of a mind processing information as it goes along. The pace
of her meditation shifts and we have the effect of an exploded pe-
riod; there is a rupture, a sense of surprise, and a shift in gram-
matical energy as Moore's metaphor emerges. Like Stevens' aes-
thetic, the snake's motion embodies both order and mystery—is
both accessible and impenetrable.

Still later in the same review Moore creates a series of meta-
phors for Stevens' harmony. The cumulative effect of these meta-
phors serves to distance us from Stevens' poetic; what appears to
be accessible is finally inscrutable.

> One has the effect of poised uninterrupted harmony, a simple
> appearing, complicated phase of symmetry of movements as in
> figure skating, tight-rope dancing, in the kaleidoscopically cen-
> trifugal circular motion of certain mediaeval dances. It recalls
> the snake in *Far Away and Long Ago*, "moving like quicksilver
> in a rope-like stream" or the conflict at sea when after a storm,
> the wind shifts and waves are formed counter to those still
> running.[48]

Moore takes us from the studied harmony of figure skating,
tight-rope dancing, and "certain mediaeval dances" to the natu-
ral, effortless grace of a snake's motion and the sea's movement
after a storm. Studied harmony can be learned or imitated in a
way that natural harmony cannot. It is the mixture of the two
kinds in Stevens which makes his project at once comprehensible
and mysterious. Once again Moore evokes a snake's motion. This
time she compares Stevens' harmony to the snake in W. H. Hud-

son's "A Serpent Mystery" in *Far Away and Long Ago*. Moore's source is worth examining:

> . . . I stood thrilled with terror, not daring to make the slightest movement, gazing down upon it. Although so long it was not a thick snake, and as it moved on over the white ground it had the appearance of a coal-black current flowing past me—a current not of water or other liquid but of some such element as quicksilver moving on in a rope-like stream. At last it vanished, and turning I fled from the ground, thinking that never again would I venture into or near that frightfully dangerous spot in spite of its fascination.[49]

Associated with mystery, danger, and the inaccessible, Hudson's serpent cannot be predicted: "dangerous on occasion as when attacked or insulted, and able in some cases to inflict death with a sudden blow, but harmless and even friendly or beneficent towards those who regarded it with kindly and reverent feelings in place of hatred."[50] Moore contains Stevens' elusiveness in her analogy as she compares his harmony to Hudson's snake, which moves "like quicksilver in a rope-like stream." She fuses the snake's inaccessibility with Stevens' in the image of quicksilver. Mercury, a liquid metal, is impossible to hold or contain unless confined to an instrument such as a thermometer or a barometer. Moore's metaphor for Stevens' enterprise momentarily contains his elusiveness; yet her metaphor itself is about the impossibility of pinning him down. Her image of quicksilver also reminds us of Stevens' mercurial temperament and her earlier contention that he shares certain affinities with the god Mercury.

Complementing the snake's coils that move in opposite directions, Moore likens Stevens' graceful harmony to "the conflict at sea when after a storm, the wind shifts and waves are formed counter to those still running." Finding an analogue for Stevens' penchant to move in contrary directions in this image of natural opposition, Moore again offers us a metaphor that controls that which cannot be predicted.

Paradoxically, the more visually precise Moore's metaphors are, the harder it is to penetrate their physics. This occurs in her 1924 review of *Harmonium*, when she addresses Stevens' "appetite for color." She focuses on a moment of great intensity that cannot possibly last.

> One is met in these poems by some such clash of pigment as where in a showman's display of orchids or gladiolas, one receives the effect of vials of picracarmine, magenta, gamboge, and violet mingled each at the highest point of intensity.[51]

The first clash we are met with is between Moore's self-effacing presence and her extravagant metaphor. Moving from simile to metaphor, as Stevens becomes first the showman with his orchids or gladiolas and then the chemist who mingles the ingredients of his vials—"each at the highest point of intensity"—Moore again gives us an image that is defined visually and aesthetically by its impermanence.

Harold Bloom maintains that Stevens "and Dickinson, more than any other Americans, more than any other moderns, labor successfully to make the visible a little hard to see."[52] I would add Moore to Bloom's list; her career as both a poet and a critic encompasses a similar quest for an affirmation that "the power of the visible / is the invisible. . . . "[53] Her tropes for Stevens' enterprise certainly mirror in their own elusiveness his labor.

We see this clearly when Moore pays tribute to Stevens' bravura in her 1937 review of *Owl's Clover*:

> But best of all, the bravura. Upon the general marine volume of statement is set a parachute-spinnaker of verbiage which looms out like half a cantaloupe and gives the body of the theme the air of a fabled argosy advancing.[54]

The movement of the sentence enacts the meaning of the meta-
phor. Moore's excessive diction unfolds like a parachute-spinnaker,
reminding us that Stevens achieves his bravura in part by in-
dulging his own penchant for extravagant language. There is
something comic in Moore's unwieldy image. Upon Stevens'
"marine volume of statement" appears a large, triangular, billowy
sail of verbiage which looms into being, taking the shape and ap-
pearance of half a cantaloupe. Moore's comparison between the
parachute-spinnaker and half a cantaloupe is visually precise,
for the shape and appearance of the melon with its ribbed rind
suggests the shape of the sail. This precision is undermined as
the spinnaker comes into sight; eluding us, it becomes trans-
formed into a fabled argosy. This classical image of a legendary
fleet of ships has a timeless fixity. We expect a complete stop at
the end of the sentence, and yet Moore's placement of the adjecti-
val modifier "advancing" subverts this expectation of closure.
Like Stevens' bravura, Moore's own excessive use of language
also sets up certain expectations only to overturn them.

In this same review Moore creates a metaphor for Stevens' elu-
sive imagery; it too comes into being only to disappear:

> This frugally unified opulence, epitomized by the "green vine
> angering for life"—in *Owl's Clover* by the thought of plundered
> harassed Africa, "the Greenest Continent" where "memory
> moves on leopard's feet"—has been perfected stroke by stroke,
> since the period of "the magenta Judas-tree," "the indigo glass
> in the grass," "oceans in obsidian," the white of "frogs," of
> "clays," and in "withered reeds"; until now, tropic pinks and
> yellows, avocado and Kuniyoshi cabouchon emerald-greens,
> the blent but violent excellence of ailanthus silk-moths and
> metallic breast-feathers—as open and unpretending as Rous-
> seau's Snake-Charmer and Sleeping Gypsy—combine in an
> impression of incandescence like that of the night-blooming
> cereus.[55]

Moore's description of the material of Stevens' poetry—of his imagery and syntactical arrangements in poems as different as "Nomad Exquisite," "The Greenest Continent," and "Primordia"—constitutes in its method of atomistically linked quotations a scarcely unified appearance of opulence. Moore asks us again to take the part or the fragment for the whole. Her quotations from *Harmonium*, *Owl's Clover*, and from Stevens' uncollected poems, such as "Primordia" and "The Indigo Glass in the Grass," coupled with her references to Kuniyoshi (a Japanese artist whose work Moore saw in 1924[56]), Rousseau, and finally the image of the night-blooming cereus (an image Moore had used in her 1924 review of *Harmonium*[57]) create a sense of visual and syntactic richness comparable to Stevens'. In fact, Moore's mosaic of perspectives here—her own carefully constructed "text"—competes with Stevens' own achievement.

Moore compares Stevens' imagery—his scarcely unified riches—to the incandescence of the night-blooming cereus. This plant blooms suddenly and unexpectedly during the night. When in bloom the flowers, which are enormous in dimension and extremely fragrant, last only a few hours. Moore's metaphor highlights the intensity and the sense of impermanence that characterize Stevens' lavish imagery. What appears to be a simile, introduced by "like," becomes a metaphor that directs our attention to the power of impermanence, change, and the shifting perspective. Like her "fabled argosy advancing," Moore's night-blooming cereus takes shape only to leave a mere trace of its presence. Moore implicitly privileges Stevens' preference for the residue that lingers after something has passed; we are reminded of Stevens' "fitful tracing of a portal" in "Peter Quince at the Clavier" or his affection for "the going of the glade-boat" in "The Load of Sugar-Cane."[58]

Her metaphor also serves to marry her aesthetic to that of Stevens'. For both of them, only that which passes can have any aesthetic permanence.[59] They both endorse what Stevens called "a

permanence composed of impermanence." In an unpublished es-
say entitled "Understatement" (dated approximately 1917–18),
Moore wrote: "Fireworks are at their best when the action is dy-
ing out of them; one might as well recognize the fact, and (often
it is that which would seem to take no precaution to be perma-
nent, which is least ephemeral.)"[60] This image anticipates the
night-blooming cereus and the "fabled argosy advancing"—two
images which Moore used in her 1937 review of *Owl's Clover* to
uncover some quality of Stevens' aesthetic only to distance us
from it.[61]

Moore's use of antithesis is still another way that she both
masks and unmasks the relationship between Stevens' aesthetic
and his temperament. Functioning as a shield for Stevens and
as a fortress for Moore as a critic, antithesis becomes a rhetori-
cal mask for both of them. For example, in the following state-
ment from her July 1925 *Dial* "Comment" we forget that Moore
is actually directing our attention to aesthetic consanguinity
when she points out that "Wallace Stevens' morosely ecstatic,
trembling yet defiant, multifarious plumage of thought and word
is to be found, also, in France."[62] To call Stevens' thought and
word "multifarious plumage" is to provide him with a kind of
armor. This armor, however, both reveals and conceals; for a
bird's plumage is both a form of protection and an unmistakable
mark of identification. Although the cadence of the two phrases—
"morosely ecstatic" and "trembling yet defiant"—suggests bal-
ance and equilibrium, both forms of antithesis imply internal di-
vision. The oxymoron "morosely ecstatic" evokes a divided self;
Stevens is both sullen and gloomy, on the one hand, and full of
rapture and passion, on the other. The second form of antithe-
sis—"trembling yet defiant"—also suggests an internal conflict.
Stevens is fearful and perhaps even subservient; he is also hostile
to authority. Moore's use of antithesis here and elsewhere in her
criticism does not merely mystify our ability to say with any
certainty what a given writer's work consists of. For Moore, Ste-

vens' artistic enterprise, and indeed any artistic endeavor, grows out of and is fueled by such divisions and struggles.

She also points to Stevens' divided self in her 1936 review of *Ideas of Order* when she directs our attention to a particularly Emersonian moment in Stevens' "Anglais Mort à Florence:"

> They [the poems in *Ideas of Order*] are a series of guarded definitions but also the unembarrassing souvenirs of a man and
>
> > '. . . the time when he stood alone,
> > When to be and delight to be seemed to be one.'[63]

Moore's description of *Ideas of Order* points to Stevens' reserve—his tendency to armor himself—and his openness to experience—to the sharing of his souvenirs.

Moore recognized from the beginning, in a way that was unparalleled among Stevens' early critics, his ability to fuse within his aesthetic "two things of opposite natures." In her 1924 review of *Harmonium*, for example, she addresses the opposition in "Sunday Morning" between "the intangible" and "the properties of the world":

> Sunday Morning . . . a poem so suggestive of a masterly equipoise—gives ultimately the effect of the mind disturbed by the intangible; of a mind oppressed by the properties of the world which it is expert in manipulating.[64]

In 1926 she also identifies Stevens' tendency to combine in one group of poems both a vision that does not seek to change its stark surroundings and a vision that insists on transforming this world:

> One recalls in "Primordia" an insisted upon starkness:
>
> > The blunt ice flows down the Mississippi,
> > At night
>
> and a complexity of apprehension:

Compilation of the effects
Of magenta blooming in the Judas-tree
And of purple blooming in the eucalyptus—[65]

Several of Moore's analogies also serve to reconcile certain op-positions in Stevens' world. In two instances her comparisons of some aspect of his poetic enterprise to an economic venture force us to reconsider Stevens' "persistent foil of dissatisfaction with matter" [66] and the impossibility of divorcing a pure aesthetic from a social and economic nexus. In both cases Moore's analogies un-dermine Stevens' ability to live in "a world elsewhere." In her 1924 review of *Harmonium*, she compares Stevens to Balzac: "The riot of gorgeousness in which Mr. Stevens' imagination takes refuge, recalls Balzac's reputed attitude to money, to which he was indifferent unless he could have it 'in heaps or by the ton.' " [67] This analogy is extravagant and comic. Balzac was ob-sessed with money, often spending in excess of what he actually possessed. Stevens, we may infer from Moore's comparison, may be "spending" in excess as well. His overactive imagination be-comes for her a kind of materialism, no less ostentatious than the worship of money.

In 1943 Moore compares Stevens to Midas: "Wallace Stevens is as susceptible to sound as objects were to Midas' golden touch." [68] Moore contends that Stevens, as an artist, is as seduced or en-slaved by sound as Midas was by his possessions. She may also be alluding to the unpleasant consequences of Midas' own suscepti-bility to sound: Midas is said to have judged a musical contest between Pan and Apollo; when he voted in favor of Pan, Apollo changed his ears to those of an ass. Midas managed to hide this fact; eventually, however, his barber noticed the transformation of his ears. Disturbed by what he had seen, the barber dug a hole in the ground where he deposited the news that Midas' ears were those of an ass. Later, when reeds grew on this spot and the wind blew through them, Midas' secret was disclosed to those who passed by. By alluding to this story, Moore may be implying that Stevens' own "secrets" are disclosed to his readers whether he wants them to be or not.

These analogies provide a more open critique of Stevens' desire to create a world apart from this one than most of Moore's other public statements do. Usually, in her reviews of Stevens, Moore conceals her ambivalence, preferring to protect Stevens' right to be aloof and inscrutable. Yet it is clear that Moore protects more than Stevens in her gestures of unmasking and masking his aesthetic. Moore protects her own poetic of disclosure and concealment—a poetic which fuels her imitative appreciation, allowing her to illuminate and compete with Stevens' own disguises.

Shortly after *Poems* (1921) was published by the Egoist Press, Moore wrote to James Sibley Watson at *The Dial* concerning an appropriate reviewer for her first book of verse: "I think after all that Wallace Stevens is so far removed that he might be the most suitable one to review my 'book.'"[69] For Moore, Stevens' detachment qualified him for the task; only someone as "far removed" as herself would be sympathetic to her own efforts. Nothing came of this suggestion because at this time Stevens did not think highly of Moore's poems. In 1922 he confided to Alice Corbin Henderson, an assistant editor of *Poetry* between 1912 and 1916 and a poet and reviewer, that he thought Moore was too concerned with "form" and with disavowing that concern.[70]

It would be thirteen years before Stevens wrote about Moore. By this time, they had corresponded and she knew from these exchanges that they were kindred spirits. Stevens published two essays about Moore's poetry. The first appeared in 1935 when he reviewed her *Selected Poems* for *Life and Letters Today*. The second one was written for the 1948 Marianne Moore issue of the *Quarterly Review of Literature*.[71] When he called Moore a "romantic" in his review of her *Selected Poems*, he implicitly examined her need to create "a world elsewhere," or, as he put it in 1948, to find "an individual reality"[72] in her surroundings.

Some time in 1935, T. C. Wilson, then associate editor of the *Westminster Magazine*, asked Stevens to review Moore's *Selected Poems*. On March 25, 1935, Stevens wrote back to Wilson, offering some preliminary observations on Moore's enterprise:

> Miss Moore is not only a complete disintegrator; she is an equally complete reintegrator. From that point of view, it would suit me very well to go over her poems, because I think that what she does is really a good deal more important than what Williams does. I cannot help feeling that Williams represents a somewhat exhausted phase of the romantic, and that his great attractiveness is due to the purity of his form.

> On the other hand, it seems to me that Miss Moore is endeavoring to create a new romantic; that the way she breaks up older forms is merely an attempt to free herself for the pursuit of the thing in which she is interested; and that the thing in which she is interested in all the strange collocations of her work is that which is essential in poetry, always: the romantic. But a fresh romantic.[73]

Wilson thought highly of Stevens' comments and wrote Moore a letter on April 9, 1935, in which he quoted at length from Stevens' letter.[74] Wilson, however, politely transcribed only part of Stevens' letter, choosing to delete Stevens' unflattering comments about Williams. Stevens had recently written the preface to Williams' *Collected Poems* (1934) and the reference he made to Williams in his letter to Wilson would not have been wasted on Moore. In his preface, which Moore knew well, having used it to frame and conclude her own review of Williams' *Collected Poems*,[75] Stevens referred to Williams as a "romantic." For Stevens, Williams' "romantic temperament" was connected to his "rejecting the accepted sense of things" and to his "sentimental side." [76] Not surprisingly, when Stevens wrote his review of Moore's *Selected Poems* a year later he was self-conscious about using the term "romantic" again. On July 12, 1935, he wrote to Wilson about the derogatory connotations the English attach to the tag: "The predominating batch today seems to think that the romantic as we know it is the slightest possible aspect of the thing. The English feel as badly about the romantic as they do about the sentimental." [77] In 1936 he wrote to Moore about this label: "I am afraid," Stevens confided, "that I shall never be able to do much with the principle that I had in mind in my note on your SELECTED POEMS so long as I stick to the use of the word *romantic*. The indelible associations of that word seem to make it impossible to use it in a fresh sense." [78] Perhaps Stevens was afraid the public would associate Moore's project with Williams'; by using the term again, he certainly invited the possibility of such a comparison. On the other hand, he may have seen this as an opportunity to hint to Williams that he might take a lesson from Moore's romanticism.

Stevens' reading of Moore's "The Steeple-Jack" does serve to revitalize the term "romantic." After singling out the "enhancing diversity" and the "sense of invigoration" in her *Selected Poems*, Stevens turns to "The Steeple-Jack" specifically. "The point of the poem," he notes, "is a view of the common-place. . . . Consciously, it may have had no more point than the wish to make note of observations made while in the cloud of a mood. That is Miss Moore's method. Subject, with her, is often incidental." [79] We are reminded of Stevens' claim in his poem "Sailing after Lunch": "It is least what one ever sees. / It is only the way one feels, to say / Where my spirit is I am." [80] Stevens abandons, as he implies Moore does in "The Steeple-Jack," the romantic project of achieving some kind of heightened vision through observation. Both writers possess an alert readiness to observe the details of their surroundings—real and imagined—with exactitude.

Moore's method depends upon a willingness to embrace the unexpected and an ability to orchestrate the details or fragments of her world; it is this process which allows her to link this world to a world of her own. Stevens points to this when he maintains:

> In *The Steeple-Jack* she observes the fog on the sea-side flowers and trees
>
> > "so that you have
> > the tropics at first hand: the trumpet vine . . .
> > or moon vines trained on fishing-twine."
>
> She then writes
>
> > ". . . There are no banyans, frangipani nor
> > jack-fruit trees; nor an exotic serpent life."
>
> If she had said in so many words that there were banyans, frangipani, and so on, she would have been romantic in the sense in which the romantic is a relic of the imagination. She hybridises the thing by a negative. That is one way. Equally she hybridises it by association. Moon-vines are moon-vines and tedious. But moon-vines trained on fishing-twine are something else and they are as perfectly as it is possible for anything to be what interests Miss Moore. They are an intermingling. The imagination grasps at such things and sates itself, instantaneously, in them.[81]

Moore forces us to see things in concert that are not usually associated with one another. She has the ability, as Stevens does, to romanticize the fragment—to make her surroundings come alive by asking us to focus on the part as a prelude to apprehending the whole. The "intermingling" Stevens refers to here could be the glimpse of the invisible Moore gives us without ever taking us out of the realm of the visible. Stevens recognizes that her fog makes the tropics both visible "at first hand" and invisible. As

Moore hybridizes or cross-fertilizes the visible and the invisible, she gives us in "The Steeple-Jack" her own version of Stevens' "method of hints and disguises," concealing as Stevens often does as much as she reveals.

Stevens did not write again about Moore's poetry after 1948. While Moore admired Stevens from the start, following his project with care and intensity between 1924 and 1964, Stevens wrote about her work only twice. To be fair, Stevens did not share Moore's commitment to reviewing the work of his contemporaries; nevertheless, he was not as consistently enthusiastic about Moore's poetry as she was about his.

3   "Firm piloting of rebellious fluency": Moore's Reviews of Pound's *Cantos*

I feel it to be the utmost generosity on the part of a critic to define even in a slight degree, the impression made by a work.[1]

By no means a chameleon, Ezra Pound wears sometimes with splendour, the cloak of mediaeval romance.[2]

A brother journal, published week-day afternoons in Denver, finds our verses, articles, and short stories, capital and a contributor—one might say a cousin, for we are less ashamed of nepotism than of seeming to quote without acknowledgement—said not long ago in the office that he was pleased we had offered The Dial Award to Ezra Pound; that Mr Pound has the intuitive mind in a degree to which few people have it, "a mind that moves back and forth like sea-weed."[3]

"An annoyance by no means petty," Moore maintains in 1931 in her first review of Ezra Pound's *Cantos*, "is the lack of an index."[4] Yet despite this complaint Moore's criticism of Pound not only does not attempt to provide an index, it thwarts, in its very method, such a systematic enterprise; in fact, her method protects Pound from those embarking on such an undertaking. "Even if one understood nothing," Moore asserts about the *Cantos*, "one would enjoy the musicianly manipulation."[5] Or as she states at the end of her second review of Pound's *Cantos* in 1934: "The test for

the *Cantos* is not obstinate continuous probing but a rereading af-
ter the interval of a year or years. . . ."[6] This seems to be Moore's
test for all of Pound's writing; essentially, her method in both
reviews of the *Cantos* charts her rereading of Pound's prose. She is
not interested in obstinate probing of individual passages or lines
from the *Cantos*, for she contends: "To cite passages is to pull one
quill from a porcupine. Mr. Pound took two thousand and more
pages to say it in prose and he sings it in a hundred-forty-two."[7]

In deference to the balance between Pound's other work and
his poetry, Moore takes us on a journey through his canon, one
that prepares us for a reading of the *Cantos* and serves to weld the
aesthetic behind his prose with that of his poetry. Moore an-
nounces that this has been her method in the last paragraph of
her 1931 review:

> Mr. Pound, in the prose that he writes, has formulated his
> own commentary upon the Cantos. They are an armorial coat
> of attitudes to things that have happened in books and in
> life; they are not a shield but a coat worn by a man, as in the
> days when heraldry was beginning. . . . His art is his turtle-
> shell or snail-house; it is all one animal moving together, and
>
>> Who seeks him must be worse than blind,
>> He and his house are so combined,
>> If finding it he fails to find
>>   its master.[8]

This single expository gesture, albeit one we might have expected
to see at the beginning of the essay, is telling, for it forces us to go
back and retrace our own movement through the essay and to
reevaluate the relationship between Pound's prose and his poetry.
Moore's extensive inventory of Pound's project traces his own
journey through literature and life, one that she explicitly argues
made *A Draft of XXX Cantos* possible. "These Cantos," Moore pro-

claims at the outset of her 1931 review, "are the epic of the far-
ings of a literary mind."[9]

Attempting to protect Pound from potentially unsympathetic
readers, Moore commits herself in both reviews to the range of
the mind and the aesthetic behind *A Draft of XXX Cantos* and the
prose/criticism Pound had written by this time. Her method of as-
sessing his aesthetic takes two forms. Moore creates an elaborate
mosaic of fragments from his prose to show us that Pound pro-
vides his own commentary on his poetic project. This method of
archaeologizing Pound's corpus necessarily highlights the frag-
ment and mirrors Pound's method in the *Cantos*. It also allows
Moore to approach Pound from her own calculated distance.
Despite Pound's many masks, however, Moore assumes, as Eliot
does, that underneath Pound's "coat" there lurks a single self.[10]

Moore also pays tribute to Pound by miming in her own rhe-
torical gestures the tensions that inform his aesthetic. Her imita-
tive appreciation of Pound serves to illuminate what for some
readers might be a potential clash between his "firm piloting"
and "rebellious fluency."[11] As with Stevens, Moore counters
Pound's obscurity with her own opacity; she also hints that de-
spite his need to be obscure and evasive he sometimes goes too
far in this direction. Her rhetorical devices shield Pound's en-
terprise from an unreceptive public as well as disguise her own
occasional ambivalence about his propensity to "'push certain
experiments beyond the right curve of their art. . . .'"[12]

Although Moore did not write her first full-length review of
Pound until 1931,[13] she usually reviewed her contemporaries
shortly after their work appeared: she reviewed Eliot's *Prufrock
and Other Observations* (1917) in 1918 for *Poetry*, *The Sacred Wood*
(1921) in 1921 for *The Dial*, Williams' *Kora in Hell* (1920) in
1921 for *Contact*, Stevens' *Harmonium* (1923) in 1924 for *The
Dial*, H.D.'s *Hymen* (1921) in 1923 for *Broom*, and *The Collected*

Poems of H.D. (1925) in 1925 for *The Dial.* That Moore did not write about Pound sooner is surprising given the fact that she first became acquainted with his work in 1909; in 1911 she purchased *Personae* (1909), *Exultations* (1909), and *Canzoni* (1911) at Elkin Mathews' Bookstore in London.[14] In addition to her London purchases, Moore owned copies of *Lustra of Ezra Pound with Earlier Poems* (1917), *Pavannes and Divisions* (1918), *Instigations* (1920), *Indiscretions; or Une Revue de Deux Mondes* (1923), and *Antheil and the Treatise on Harmony* (1924).[15] Her consistent attention to Pound's work during the late teens and twenties can also be documented by occasional references to him in essays she wrote; in addition, their correspondence during these decades shows that they were each interested in what the other was doing. In 1918, Pound wrote a brief statement for the *Little Review* on Moore and Mina Loy; although he was condescending and his analysis of their work lacked focus, Pound probably believed he had made a genuine effort to gain some attention for their respective poetic projects.[16] In 1919, Pound suggested that he try to publish a volume of Moore's verse for her. Moore appreciated Pound's offer but declined to avail herself of his suggestion. In the twenties he wrote to her asking to be apprised of "how things are in N.Y."[17] Over the years they exchanged many letters on this topic and others, though they did not actually meet until 1939.

The *Dial* correspondence during Moore's tenure as editor (1925–1929) documents her commitment to Pound's enterprise, particularly his work as an editor and as a critic. Moore solicited prose and poetry from Pound; she also regarded him as a surrogate editor. It was Pound, for example, who advised her to publish Cheever Dunning, Louis Zukofsky, and De Schloezer.[18] It was also during Moore's tenure as editor that Pound received the 1927 *Dial* Award.[19] It is possible that she was reticent to write about Pound until she could firmly establish what his work as a whole exemplified. She may also have felt that to consider all of Pound's work in concert would be the greatest tribute she could provide. When she wrote about Henry James in 1934, she attempted to do the same thing; both essays survey and orchestrate quotations from much of the work each writer had produced.

Her first review of *A Draft of XXX Cantos* was the longest review *Poetry* had ever published.[20] In fact, it was the longest review Moore wrote of any of the moderns. The elaborate parquetlike effect of quotations from Pound's *How to Read, Instigations, Lustra, Pavannes and Divisions, The Spirit of Romance,* and *A Draft of XXX Cantos,* as well as from reviews by Eliot and Williams, indicates the extent to which Moore, in her first review of the *Cantos,* was taking stock of Pound's enterprise as a whole. (In the essay there were so many unidentified quotations from Pound's earlier work, particularly his prose, that Harriet Monroe, the editor of *Poetry,* out of deference to Moore's readers, added a footnote at the beginning of the essay, clarifying when a reader might assume Moore was quoting from the *Cantos* and when from Pound's other work.)

When Moore reviewed the *Cantos* in the thirties, critics were divided about the value of his project. In retrospect, the whole decade seems overshadowed by Yeats' articulate and elegant disparagement of Pound's *Cantos,* which appeared in his 1936 introduction to *The Oxford Book of Modern Verse:*

> Ezra Pound has made flux his theme; plot, characterization, logical discourse, seem to him abstractions unsuitable to a man of his generation. . . . The relation of all the elements to one another, repeated or unrepeated, is to become apparent when the whole is finished. There is no transmission through time, we pass without comment from ancient Greece to modern England, from modern England to medieval China; the symphony, the pattern, is timeless, flux eternal and therefore without movement. Like other readers I discover at present merely exquisite or grotesque fragments. He hopes to give the impression that all is living, that there are no edges, no con-

vexities, nothing to check the flow; but can such a poem have
a mathematical structure? Can impressions that are in part
visual, in part metrical, be related like the notes of a sym-
phony. . . ? Style and its opposite can alternate, but form must
be full, spherelike, single. . . . Even where the style is sustained
throughout one gets an impression, especially when he is writ-
ing in *vers libre*, that he has not got all the wine into the bowl,
that he is a brilliant improvisator translating at sight from an
unknown Greek masterpiece. . . .[21]

Yeats' assessment of Pound's ambitious project, Pound later said,
did "more to prevent people [from] reading [the] Cantos for what
is 'on the page' than any other . . . smoke screen."[22] (Walter
Sutton maintains that Yeats' "reaction is typical of many British
readers and writers, who have tended to distrust free verse pat-
terns and experimental techniques."[23])

In contrast, Pound's American readers, Eliot, Williams, Moore,
Delmore Schwartz, R. P. Blackmur, and Allen Tate, tended to em-
brace his many carefully carved fragments.[24] Although written
five years before Yeats' introduction to *The Oxford Book of Modern
Verse*, Williams' review of Pound's *Draft of XXX Cantos* in April of
1931 provides, in retrospect, the kind of defense Pound would
need after what he referred to as "Yeats' bloody paragraph."[25]
Williams' review, entitled appropriately "Excerpts from a Critical
Sketch: *A Draft of XXX Cantos* by Ezra Pound," counters the re-
sponse typified by Yeats' impatience with Pound's transmission of
flux, his fragments, and his lack of "edges [or] convexities." Wil-
liams, who in 1925 praised Moore's poetic enterprise and the
modern one in general for embodying "a break *through* all pre-
conceptions of poetic form and mood and pace, a flaw, a crack in
the bowl,"[26] certainly understood in a way that Yeats did not that
Pound intentionally resisted a vision that hoped to get all the
wine into the bowl.

In this unorthodox review, Williams' fragments of apprecia-

tion champion and mirror Pound's fragments and seemingly
unhinged juxtapositions in the *Cantos*. Praising Pound's "shot
through all material" as he had Moore's "anthology of transit"
six years before,[27] Williams opposes those who wish for a synthe-
sis of Pound's material:

> Only superficially do the *Cantos* fuse the various temporal
> phases of the material Pound has chosen, into a synthesis. It is
> important to stress this for it is Pound's chief distinction in the
> *Cantos*—his personal point of departure from most that the
> modern is attempting. It is not by any means a synthesis, but a
> shot through all material—a true and somewhat old-fashioned
> analysis of his world.[28]

Williams may have been trying to separate Pound's method from
Eliot's, and thus may have gone out of his way to claim that
Pound's enterprise in the *Cantos* did not resemble those of the
other moderns.[29]

In her first review of Pound's *Cantos*, Moore alludes to Wil-
liams' argument that Pound gives his readers a "somewhat old-
fashioned analysis of his world." Citing both Eliot and Williams,
Moore offers her own analysis of what is outdated in Pound:

> T. S. Eliot suspects Mr. Pound's philosophy of being anti-
> quated. W.C. Williams finds his "versification *still* patterned af-
> ter classic metres"; and, apropos of 'feminolatry,' is not the
> view of woman expressed by the Cantos older-fashioned than
> that of Siam and Abyssinia? knowledge of the femaleness of
> "chaos," of the "octopus," of "Our mulberry leaf, woman," ap-
> pertaining more to the Grand Turk than to a Roger Ascham?[30]

Comparing Pound's view of woman to that held by those in the
East and Africa (Siam was the former name of Thailand and
Abyssinia the former name of Ethiopia), Moore censors Pound
for his backward "feminolatry." The references to Canto XXIX
also criticize Pound, for in this canto man's "feminolatry" consists

of desire which is often thwarted by woman, who is "a chaos,"
"an octopus," and "a biological process." She is also dependent
and in need of education: "She seeking a guide, a mentor, / He
aspires to a career with honour." And Pound, Moore suggests, is
not Roger Ascham, the Renaissance educator.

In still another overt criticism of Pound, Moore also cites
Williams:

> And in all this 'wealth of motive,' this '*largesse,*' this 'intel-
> ligence,' are there no flaws? Does every passage in this sym-
> phony 'relieve, refresh, revive the mind of the reader—at
> reasonable intervals—with some form of ecstasy, by some
> splendor of thought, some presentation of sheer beauty, some
> lightning turn of phrase'? Not invariably. The "words affect
> modernity," says William Carlos Williams, "with too much
> violence (at times)—a straining after slang effects. . . ." "You
> cannot *easily* switch from Orteum to Peoria without violence (to
> the language). These images too greatly infest the Cantos."[31]

Moore uses Williams here to support her own belief that Pound
occasionally moves too quickly between the classical world and
the contemporary, or between a formal discourse and a casual
conversation.

When Moore sent Williams the proof of her review in 1931—
she reviewed the *Cantos* six months after Williams did—she
praised his review: "It is so good it seemed to me there was noth-
ing more to say, but I had gone some distance, so continued."[32]
Moore's contention that perhaps she had nothing to add to Wil-
liams' pronouncements suggests a dependence on Williams that
is belied by her forty-eight pages of manuscript notes for her re-
view and the review itself.[33] While Williams and Moore both em-
ploy imitative appreciation in their respective pieces, Moore did
not learn this technique from Williams. Most important, how-
ever, Williams restricts himself to a discussion of Pound's *Cantos*

whereas Moore insists on considering the full range of Pound's venture in both his prose and his poetry. More than anyone else who wrote on Pound, certainly before Eliot's retrospective essay on Pound in 1946 and Hugh Kenner's monumental study, *The Poetry of Ezra Pound* (1951),[34] Moore understood and explored the relationship between Pound's prose and his poetry. For Moore, Pound's *Cantos* were a watershed in his career because they crystallized and compressed an aesthetic that he had been defining in his many pages of prose.

In her 1931 review, Moore also focuses on Pound's skill or "ambidextrous precision"—his ability to be vague and yet precise in this endeavor—in her discussion of his criticism and translations, two endeavors that she feels inform Pound's *Cantos*. We notice here that Moore weaves into her own text two statements from his *Pavannes and Divisions*; by doing this, she allows Pound the opportunity to provide his own commentary on, and defense of, his aesthetic preferences.

> The skill that in the prose has been incomparably expert in epitomizing what others have bungled, shows us that 'you can be wholly precise in representing a vagueness.' This ambidextrous precision, born of integrity and intrepidity, is the poet's revenge upon those 'who refuse to say what they think, if they do think—' who are like those who see nothing the matter with bad surgery. And allied with veracity are translatory qualities that nourish ingenuity in the possessor of them: a so unmixed zeal for essence that no assaying of merits in rendering is a trouble; an independence that will not subscribe to superstition—to the notion, for instance, that a text written in Greek is of necessity better than a text written in Latin. Even Homer can be put characteristically into Latin.[35]

Moore's assumption that Pound's role as a critic is inseparable from his role as a poet was a much more radical position for her to take then than it would be today, inasmuch as contemporary criticism forces us to break down the distinction between the critic and the artist. For although Eliot could say in "The Perfect Critic" that "the two directions of sensibility are complementary" and that "it is to be expected that the critic and creative artist should frequently be the same person,"[36] he seldom wavers from valuing the creative enterprise over the critical.

In the 1940s and 1950s the trend was not to see the critic and the poet as one and the same. Kenner begins his study of Pound in 1951 by defensively maintaining: "To the stereoscopic gaze of plenary critical judgment Pound the critic and Pound the poet are the same organism. The cross-eyed supposition that we are in the presence of two unblended functions breeds nothing but confusion."[37] Moore had also acknowledged this twenty years before Kenner did. "Mr. Pound, in the prose that he writes," Moore asserted in 1931, "has formulated his own commentary upon the Cantos."

Moore's training to read Pound's *Cantos* does not merely include her reading of his prose. She also pays close attention to criticism of Pound. Eliot, whose writing on Pound Moore knew well, was an important precursor of her ideas about him, although her method of approaching Pound does not resemble Eliot's expository analysis of his project. Based on Moore's references to Eliot's criticism in her manuscript notes for her 1931 review of the *Cantos*,[38] we can see that for her Eliot becomes a kind of mediator between herself and Pound, providing her with assumptions and questions against which she can measure her own.

Moore was influenced by Eliot's "The Method of Mr. Pound" which was published in *The Athenaeum* in 1919. In her copy of *Personae* we find the following note in the back:

> Review of Propertius Athenaeum 24 Oct TSE still struggling beneath enormous weight 31 Oct of granite laurels wherewith the immortal author etc. . . .[39]

On October 24, 1919, Eliot had reviewed Pound's *Quia Pauper Amavi*, which contained "Homage to Sextus Propertius," and a week later, on October 31, 1919, Pound wrote a letter to the editor of *The Athenaeum* commenting on Eliot's review. Pound begins his letter by saying that he is "still struggling beneath the enormous weight of granite laurels wherewith the immortal author of 'Sweeny [*sic*] among the Nightingales' has so generously loaded [his] superstructure. . . . "[40] Moore's references to both Eliot's review and Pound's response exemplify her early interest in Pound's fate at the hands of Eliot and his weighty laurels.

In this review, Eliot focuses on Pound's "deliberate and conscious method," maintaining that "Mr. Pound's early work, taken by itself, might give the impression of being a brilliant and immensely appreciative piece of archaeology"[41]; but, he concludes, Pound's collection of fragments is not merely a collection of disparate shards that reveal a broken, necessarily incomplete knowledge of the past:

> Mr. Pound's method is indirect and one extremely difficult to pursue. . . . Mr. Pound proceeds by acquiring the entire past; and when the entire past is acquired, the constituents fall into place and the present is revealed.[42]

In 1931, Moore asserts: "You must read it [*A Draft of XXX Cantos*] yourself; it has the surging of power that is mind and is music; it comes with the impact of centuries and with the impact of yesterday."[43] Moore's interest in the balance between the distant past and the immediate past in Pound's work echoes Eliot's earlier assertion.

Eliot maintains in 1919 that Pound "must hide to reveal himself. But if we collate all these disguises we find not a mere collection of green-room properties, but Mr. Pound."[44] This belief lays the groundwork for the kind of argument Moore will make at the end of her 1931 review. Like Eliot, who had called the *Cantos* "an objective and reticent autobiography,"[45] Moore also subscribes to the belief that behind Pound's many masks is one person.

In 1918, in "Ezra Pound: His Metric and Poetry," Eliot argued that Pound's early work constituted a preparation for the *Cantos*:

> We will leave it as a test: when anyone has studied Mr. Pound's poems in *chronological* order, and has mastered *Lustra* and *Cathay*, he is prepared for the *Cantos*—but not till then. If the reader then fails to like them, he has probably omitted some step in his progress, and had better go back and retrace the journey.[46]

We know from Moore's references to Eliot's essay in her manuscript notes for her 1931 review of Pound that she had read this essay with considerable care.[47] Eliot's advice may have encouraged her to retrace her own journey through Pound before writing on his *Draft of XXX Cantos*. Not surprisingly, Moore also stresses the continuity between Pound's earlier poems and the *Cantos*:

> Those who object to the poem's obscurity—who prefer the earlier poems—are like the victims of Calvin who have not read him. It may be true that the author's revisions make it harder, not easier, for hurried readers; but flame kindles to the eye that contemplates it.[48]

Eliot's greatest contribution to Moore's reading of Pound, however, can be seen in the way he accounts for "the 'freedom' of [Pound's] verse," for what Moore will later call Pound's "love of risk":

> So much for the imagery. As to the 'freedom' of his verse, Pound has made several statements in his articles on Dolmetsch which are to the point:
> 'Any work of art is a compound of freedom and order. It is perfectly obvious that art hangs between chaos on the one side

and mechanics on the other. A pedantic insistence upon detail tends to drive out 'major form.' A firm hold on major form makes for a freedom of detail. In painting men intent on minutiae gradually lost the sense of form and form-combination. An attempt to restore this sense is branded as 'revolution.' It is revolution in the philological sense of the term . . .

'Art is a departure from fixed positions; felicitous departure from a norm. . . .'[49]

In her manuscript notes for her 1931 review of the *Cantos* Moore cites three of these statements and the page on which they appeared in Eliot's essay:

> art is a compound of freedom and order
>
> 15   firm hold on major form makes for a freedom of detail
>
> Pound Art is a departure fr fixed positions,
> felicitous departure fr fixed positions;
> felicitous departure fr a norm.[50]

Given other phrases that are underlined in her manuscript notes and later incorporated into her text, we can conjecture that she may have considered using these statements in the same manner. They do not appear in either of her reviews, but in both essays she certainly pays tribute to the aesthetic embodied in them.

Moore's rhetorical gestures can be seen as a synthesis of freedom and order, embodying Pound's dictum that "art is a departure from fixed positions." For Pound, all art involves both the creation of a pattern and the breaking of that pattern; a flaw in the form enables us to re-imagine the form. Moore seeks to re-create the effect of Pound's poetic in her own stylistic excursions, mirroring in her own style Pound's "love of risk,"[51] his "descriptive exactness,"[52] his ability to fuse that which is heard with that which is seen, and "his 'freedom of motion' in saying what he has to say 'like a bolt from a catapult.'"[53]

Two of Moore's images in her 1931 review of the *Cantos*, that of a mediaeval dance and a rampant horse, function as metaphors for Pound's reverence for the unpredictable, for the way that the departure from the predictable can be accommodated by the whole:

> But however explicit the accents in the line, always the fabric on which the pattern is focussed is indispensable to accurate rendering. There is the effect sometimes, as in the mediaeval dance, of a wheel spun one way and then the other; there is the sense of a horse rushing toward one and turning, unexpectedly rampant; one has stepped back but need not have moved.[54]

Moore uses the mediaeval dance as a metaphor for Pound's aesthetic because of the way the form allows people to be unpredictable in predictable ways, to shift from one sort of movement or pace to another without violating the dance as a whole. Curt Sachs notes in his *World History of the Dance* that a single mediaeval dance allowed for "restrained marching," "gliding," and "free, spirited skipping and leaping."[55] Pound's rhythm in the *Cantos* can also accommodate such shifts in pace without disturbing "the fabric on which the pattern is focussed." We can also see a blending of Pound's freedom and order in Moore's image of a rampant horse rushing toward one. Again we have a form, in this case a ritual of some sort, that allows for a departure from the expected. This unexpected shift in expectation, however, does not upset the equilibrium of the whole. Moore shows that there is, after all, only the appearance of danger or disorder: a shift in positions was unnecessary.

In this same review she describes Pound's "facing in many directions" in the *Cantos*; here her imitative appreciation praises and undermines Pound's penchant for taking risks:

'All artists who discover anything . . . must, in the course of things, . . . push certain experiments beyond the right curve of their art,' Mr. Pound says, and some would say, the facing in many directions as of a quadriga drawn by centaurs, that we meet in the Cantos, puts strain on bipedal understanding; there is love of risk; but the experienced grafting of literature upon music is here very remarkable—the resonance of color, allusions, tongues, sounding each through the other as in symphonic instrumentation.[56]

Dropping out of sight momentarily, Moore again uses Pound to comment on his own project; this time she quotes Pound on Henry James. This gesture would not have been wasted on Pound, for in his essay on James, Pound had endorsed James' excesses and need to push beyond his method:

All artists who discover anything make such detours and must, in the course of things (as in the cobwebs), push certain experiments beyond the right curve of their art. This is not so much the doom as the function of all 'revolutionary' or experimental art, and I think master-work is usually the result of the return from such excess. One does not know, simply does not know, the true curve until one has pushed one's method beyond it. Until then it is merely a frontier, not a chosen route.[57]

By quoting from this passage Moore endorses Pound's need to take the risks he does in the *Cantos*. She also unharnesses her own "love of risk" as her image of a quadriga drawn by centaurs emerges in the middle of her lengthy but controlled sentence. This obscure image becomes a parody of Pound's inclination to extend himself in several directions at once and to move beyond the boundaries his art might cultivate. There is something incongruous about this image. A quadriga (a chariot drawn by four horses harnessed abreast) suggests fixity, because depictions of quadrigas are usually found on coins or in sculpture. This static image is however belied by the presence of centaurs, mythological creatures notable for their ability to face in many, often contradictory directions, and for their skills in music, medicine, hunting, and prophecy. In Pound's essay "The Serious Artist," we find: "Poetry is a centaur. The thinking word-arranging, clarifying faculty must move and leap with the energizing, sentient, musical faculties."[58] Moore's manuscript notes for this review indicate that this passage was the source for her extravagant metaphor.[59]

In her 1934 review of the *Cantos*, Moore's own verbal acrobatics also rival Pound's:

> His [Pound's] feeling for verse above prose—that for prose 'a much greater amount of language is needed than for poetry'—is like Schönberg's statement: 'My greatest desire is to compress the most substance into the least possible space,' and Stravinsky's trick of ending a composition with the recoil of a good ski-jumper accepting a spill.[60]

What appears to be a simple analogy between Pound's preference for compression and that of Schönberg, leads to Moore's own exuberant metaphor for compression. Her marshalling of quotations from first Pound and then Schönberg creates a mask for her and leaves us unprepared for what follows. As Moore reasserts her own presence, her metaphor constitutes a departure from the limits she has set up in the first part of the sentence. We expect an end stop after Schönberg's statement, but instead are presented with a conjunction that unexpectedly launches Moore's imitative appreciation of Pound's compression. The conjunction signals a shift in pace and a division between the first part of the sentence and Moore's metaphor. The structure of the sentence, then, complements the tension in Pound between the fixed and the departure from it.

Moore's pitting the discourse of music against the discourse of athletics verges on the parodic. Imitating Pound's compression, she fuses what is heard (Stravinsky's composition) with what is seen ("a good ski-jumper accepting a spill"). We can see Stravinsky's composition end with the same clarity that we can envision a good ski-jumper's fall. Conversely, Moore makes us hear the ski-jumper's spill with the same intensity that we can hear Stravinsky's ending. We notice that Stravinsky's endings are likened to a ski-jumper's spill and not a jump; Moore focuses on a moment of interruption or rupture. Stravinsky's compositions end unexpectedly just as the ski-jumper's failed, yet accepted, gesture occurs unexpectedly. Moore would argue that Stravinsky's compositions—like Pound's *Cantos*—have built into their form the possibility for these ruptures or departures from the fixed position. Similarly, the ski-jumper's spill cannot be predicted, yet the act of jumping always allows for its possibility. In both instances, Moore focuses on what Williams refers to as "a flaw, a crack in the bowl." Finally it is the unexpected, or the rupture in the form or ritual, which allows us to reaffirm the possibility of the whole.

Moore also makes us both see and hear Pound's fusion of rhetoric and sound: "The edges of the rhetoric and of sound are well 'luted,' as in good lacquer-work, and the body throughout is ennobled by insinuated rhyme effects and a craftily regulated tempo."[61] The verb "to lute" means to treat with "lute," a composition for making joints airtight. Moore's verb as well as her analogy between Pound's craft and the craft of furniture-making thus visually joins Pound's rhetoric and sound. The image of lacquer-work also reminds us of the layers of masks and discourses in the *Cantos*.

Moore captures the movement of Pound's verse in her visually precise description of his rhythm and "sustained emphasis."

'The heart is the form,' as is said in the East—in this case the rhythm which is a firm piloting of rebellious fluency; the

> quality of sustained emphasis, as of a cargo being shrewdly
> steered to the edge of the quai.[62]

The clash between the phrases "firm piloting" and "rebellious
fluency" emphasizes the tension in Pound's work between the
whole form and the attendant details. When Moore describes
Pound's rhythm she makes Pound into a pilot who controls that
which appears to be unmanageable or refractory. The second part
of the sentence builds on the discourse of piloting with its more
extended metaphor; Moore likens the quality of Pound's empha-
sis to "a cargo being shrewdly steered to the edge of the quai."
Her metaphor welds form and content: a cargo contains goods
and thus the content of the cargo is at stake if the steering is not
shrewd. In both parts of the sentence, Moore implicitly stresses
Pound's skill in firm piloting and shrewd steering in an effort,
perhaps, to defend him from those who see only discontinuous
fragments.

Moore, however, is equally capable of subtly undermining
Pound's enterprise. We see this in her 1934 review of the *Cantos*
in which she compares " 'the usual subjects of conversation' " in
the *Cantos* to a grasshopper-wing:

> We have in them 'the usual subjects of conversation between
> intelligent men'—'books, arms . . . men of unusual genius,
> both of ancient times and our own'—arranged in the style of
> the grasshopper-wing for contrast, half the fold against the
> other half, the rarefied effect against a greyer one.[63]

Moore may be echoing Allen Tate's remarks about Pound's
Cantos. "The secret of his form," Tate writes in *The Nation* in
1931, "is this: conversation. The *Cantos* are talk, talk, talk; not by
anyone in particular; they are just rambling talk."[64] Moore in-
vites us to notice the arrangement of these " 'subjects of conversa-
tion,' " by fusing in her image of the grasshopper-wing what is
heard with what is seen. Her image suggests the extent to which

we have the illusion of a conversation in the *Cantos*; grasshoppers have two sets of wings: forewings and hind wings. The forewings are leathery in texture, and when the insect is in repose they cover and conceal the hind wings. Both pairs of wings, however, are used when the grasshopper flies; the two sets of wings, like Pound's conversation, function as one. We can also hear the buzz of Moore's insect; as grasshoppers fly they often produce a mechanical sound or a crackling noise that is caused by one pair of wings touching the other. Thus Moore's image of Pound's "rambling talk" may be less complimentary than her precise image might suggest.

On another level, however, her image defends Pound from those who see no connection between the part, the isolated fragment, and the whole. Her microscopic examination of the grasshopper-wing rather than the whole form pays homage, in its precision, to Pound's reverence for "the applicability of scientific method to literary criticism." [65] Moore's image of the grasshopper-wing becomes a trope about form in the same way that Pound's anecdote in *ABC of Reading* about Agassiz and the fish is:

> The proper METHOD for studying poetry and good letters is the method of contemporary biologists, that is careful first-hand examination of the matter, and continual COMPARISON of one 'slide' or specimen with another.
>
> No man is equipped for modern thinking until he has understood the anecdote of Agassiz and the fish:
>
> A post-graduate student equipped with honours and diplomas went to Agassiz to receive the final and finishing touches. The great man offered him a small fish and told him to describe it.
>
> Post-Graduate Student: 'That's only a sunfish.'
>
> Agassiz: 'I know that. Write a description of it.'
>
> After a few minutes the student returned with the descrip-

tion of the Ichthus Heliodiplodokus, or whatever term is used
to conceal the common sunfish from vulgar knowledge, family
of Heliichtherinkus, etc., as found in textbooks of the subject.
   Agassiz again told the student to describe the fish.
   The student produced a four-page essay. Agassiz then told
him to look at the fish. At the end of three weeks the fish was
in an advanced state of decomposition, but the student knew
something about it.[66]

I quote at such length from Pound because of the modernist
aesthetic implicit in this anecdote. Agassiz teaches Pound that all
knowledge is necessarily fragmented and does not constitute a
whole. Only by careful study of the part—by looking closely at
one part and comparing it to another—can we approximate a
perception of the whole form. The fish cannot be known until it
has begun to rot or decay—to separate into its elements. Knowl-
edge is broken, fragmented, and momentary.

Moore's two reviews of Pound's *Draft of XXX Cantos* also privi-
lege the fragment. Dispensing with all expository conventions,
she abandons transitions between and within paragraphs. As
my reading suggests, the sentence, and sometimes the phrase, is
Moore's unit. Her transit through Pound takes us at a dizzying
pace not only through and around the *Cantos*, but through much
of Pound's other writing up to this time. Moore's translations of
his aesthetic serve to protect him from those who see merely
"talk, talk, talk," as Tate did, or "a brilliant improvisator" who
"has not got all the wine into the bowl," as Yeats did. Her impro-
visations are also designed to remind Pound that his unpredict-
able excursions from the predictable were occasionally excessive.

4 "Poets are never of the world in which they live": Moore's Quarrel with Williams

> If I am obstructing William Carlos Williams it is through a genius for helping by hindering, as I am disturbing the quiet of the home just now by trying to write on his Collected Poems.[1]

In *I Wanted to Write a Poem* (1958), William Carlos Williams noted somewhat defensively that some of his critics had reacted unfavorably to Book Four of *Paterson:*

> My critics, Randall Jarrell among them—and Marianne Moore had the same reaction—felt that Book Four was less expert than the earlier parts of the poem. It was not as acceptable to them, I believe, because the material I was dealing with was not perceptive. But the poem in Book Four is the same poem as it was in Book One. To have a moral reaction to this section of the poem because I have seen what I have seen is just too bad.[2]

Despite Williams' claim to the contrary, Jarrell's and Moore's responses to his work clearly meant a great deal to him. According to Williams, Jarrell "admired the first two books of *Paterson,* [but] didn't react at all to Book Four. . . ."[3] We cannot, however, reconstruct Williams' critical reception based on his memory here, for Jarrell did in fact comment on Book Four of *Paterson* in *Partisan Review* in 1951:

Now that Book IV has been printed, one can come to some conclusions about *Paterson* as a whole. My first conclusion is this: it doesn't seem to be a whole; my second: *Paterson* has been getting rather steadily worse. Most of Book IV is much worse than II and III, and neither of them even begins to compare with Book I. Book IV is so disappointing that I do not want to write about it at any length: it would not satisfactorily conclude even a quite mediocre poem. Both form and content often seem a parody of those of the 'real' *Paterson*; many sections have a scrappy inconsequence, an arbitrary irrelevance, that is extraordinary; poetry of the quality of that in Book I is almost completely lacking. . . .[4]

Jarrell's contention that *Paterson* did not hold together as a whole must have been hard for Williams to hear. In 1946 Jarrell had reviewed Book One of *Paterson* and had exclaimed: "*Paterson* (Book I) seems to me the best thing William Carlos Williams has ever written; I read it seven or eight times, and ended up lost in delight."[5] Thinking of Williams' projected three books, Jarrell ended on this note: "There has never been a poem more American . . . if the next three books are as good as this one . . . the whole poem will be far and away the best long poem any American has written."[6] Yet, by 1951, it was precisely "the whole poem" that Jarrell could not approach.

Jarrell's response to *Paterson* in 1951 could have been predicted, however, given his 1949 introduction to Williams' *Selected Poems*.[7] Although Jarrell praises Williams, he refuses to ignore "Williams' bad poems" which "are usually rather winning machine-parts minus their machine, irrepressible exclamations about the weather of the world, interesting but more or less autonomous and irrelevant entries in a Lifetime Diary."[8] Jarrell's desire to see the machine—to see *Paterson* as a whole—and not a series of machine-parts made him judge the unevenness of Williams' most ambitious project with severity.

Marianne Moore, who was certainly not known for the kind of analysis Jarrell practiced, was also acutely aware of Williams' unevenness and his tendency toward, to use Stevens' phrase, "incessant new beginnings."[9] In May of 1951 Barbara Asch wrote to her from New Directions to ask for a statement concerning Book Four of Williams' *Paterson*. Moore wrote back: "Not much help this time I'm afraid."[10] Her public silence on this score, however, did not extend to her private correspondence with Williams. In June of 1951, Williams and Moore exchanged several letters on the subject of Book Four of *Paterson*. On June 19 Williams wrote to Moore to defend his world—though he claimed not to—and implied that Moore did not inhabit it.

> To me the normal world is something which to you must seem foreign. I won't defend my world. I live in it. Those I find there have all the qualities which inform those about them who are luckier. I rather like my old gal who appears in the first pages of Paterson IV (if she's one of the things you object to) she has a hard part to play and to my mind plays it rather well.[11]

In her response on June 22 Moore begged the question of which world either of them lived in and turned her attention instead to the world of *Paterson*:

> The trouble for me with your rough and ready girl, is that she does not seem to me part of something that is inescapably typical. That is to say, writing is not just virtuosity; but an interpretation of life—protest as you may in the style of our early arguments about the lily and the mud. (One as "lovely" technically speaking, as the other!)
> And I take it hard that the technical achievement here, in Paterson IV, *is* [Moore's emphasis] achievement in the early parts, and useful to me. (Ponder this if you will.)[12]

"The lily and the mud" did not enjoy equal places in Moore's scheme. For someone who valued aesthetic consistency above all, Williams' new beginning in Book Four, his "rough and ready girl," threatened to negate for Moore the technical excellence that she found in this book as well as the earlier ones.

It was late in Williams' career before he publicly acknowledged the extent to which Moore differed from him; when he did this, he singled out her private criticism of him rather than her public reviews of his work:

> Marianne Moore has always been very out-spoken in her criticisms of me in private letters. Technically, she doesn't see eye to eye with me. She's a splendid poet in her own right.[13]

Moore's criticisms of Williams were not confined to private letters. Frequently she also expressed them in her reviews, but her method was such that her criticism could always be disguised or veiled. Moore chose to disguise her ambivalence about Williams' enterprise because of her conviction that criticism—introductions, prefaces, and reviews of one's contemporaries—ought both to champion and to protect the writer under consideration.[14] Thus when she approached Williams' work, particularly after her 1921 review of *Kora in Hell*, Moore praised certain aspects of his work but felt compelled to veil her increasing dissatisfaction with his aesthetic.

I begin with Moore's private reaction to *Paterson*—one that is not in fact incompatible with her public reviews—because to date more attention has been paid to the way they saw "eye to eye" with one another. It has been assumed that Moore's response to *Paterson* was a departure from her earlier reception of his work. In this instance, however, Moore privately articulated an uneasiness with Williams that she had publicly masked over the years in her reviews. After she reviewed *Kora in Hell* in 1921, Moore increasingly approached Williams' work with reservations, but she disguised them, in part by using Stevens as a mask. When she reviewed Williams' *Collected Poems 1921–1931* in 1934, for example, Moore used Stevens' preface to Williams' *Collected Poems* to frame her own reading, a reading that both supports Stevens' and departs from it. Stevens' perception of "the constant interaction of two opposites"[15] in Williams was in keeping with Moore's own perception of this quality in *Kora in Hell*. But, more important, Stevens became a mask for her, allowing her to disguise her own struggle with Williams by ostensibly paying homage to Stevens' reading.

Williams himself wanted to believe, at least up to 1925, that Moore, unlike most of his contemporaries, shared his aesthetic values. In 1916 he wrote to Moore and asked her for a contribution to *Others*. He also indicated that he hoped they would meet soon.[16] The same year Moore wrote to H.D. at *The Egoist* and indicated that she was "very much interested . . . in William Williams' work but . . . a little afraid to undertake a criticism of it. I feel," she confided, "that I have not seen enough of it to justify my writing one."[17]

In 1917, the year Williams paid his first visit to Moore, who was then living in Chatham, N.J., he consulted her about the appropriateness of the title for his third book of poems. According to Paul Mariani, Williams had thought of calling it *Pagan Promises* but "was [now] thinking of calling it *Al Que Quiere!*, since foreign titles for books were in just then. . . ."[18] Apparently Williams had to convince his publisher that the new title would be better, for Moore wrote to him: "I am glad to be asked to assist you in overbearing on your publisher for there is no doubt in my mind that *Al Que Quiere* is the better title for the book. *Al Que Quiere* is succinct and a beautiful title."[19]

When *Kora in Hell* was published, Williams turned again to Moore; this time he asked her to review it.[20] Her review was published in 1921 in *Contact*. Two years later in 1923 Williams wrote an essay about Moore which he sent to her in December of that year:

> Read this and comment if you care to. I am revising the other
> copy—which I have made. I wrote to Elliot [*sic*] telling him he
> will received ["d" crossed out by hand] the finished work in a
> week or so. Hope he ["he" handwritten] prints it, for your sake—
> and for mine. If he doesn't we'll have it appear, even if it must
> be in BROOM. Would that shock you?[21]

According to Mariani, Williams intended to send his essay to
The Dial, but decided not to when he saw Eliot's short review of
Moore's *Poems* and "Marriage" in the December issue of *The Dial*.
Instead, he sent it to Eliot, hoping that Eliot would publish it in
The Criterion.[22] Nothing came of this effort.

In February of 1924 Williams wrote to Moore from Europe to
suggest that she publish a book of her poems with the Contact
Press that "would have my appreciation of you as a preface." "We
would want it," he continued, "to include *everything* [Williams'
emphasis] of yours that you find good from the beginning up to
the present."[23] Although Williams and Robert McAlmon were
unable to convince Moore to publish a volume with their press,
Williams succeeded in publishing his critical essay about Moore
the following year; it appeared in 1925 in *The Dial*.

During these early years Williams championed Moore and al-
lied his own aesthetic with hers in both *Spring and All* (1923) and
his 1925 essay, "Marianne Moore." Moore also began her pro-
motion of Williams, but this enterprise was fraught with reserva-
tions. Moore's reception of Williams begins with her 1921 review
of *Kora in Hell*. It is not surprising that Williams asked her to re-
view *Kora in Hell*, for he clearly identified with her aesthetic and
had reason to believe she would be sympathetic to his project.
When he saw the review, however, he hesitated about publishing
it in *Contact*. On March 27, 1921, Moore wrote to H.D. about
the review and indicated that Williams had reservations about
using it in *Contact*:

I told William that I would review KORA IN HELL since he wished it, for CONTACT. I have just sent him the review and in writing me about it, he suggests that I send it to THE BOOK-MAN; he speaks heartily of it but evidently does not think of using it in CONTACT, so that I fear you may not see it if I do not send you a copy.[24]

Williams did in fact publish this review in *Contact*, but when he responded privately to the review, he stressed Moore's criticism of his work. After an initial burst of enthusiasm for the review—"You make the blood to flow in my smallest capillaries again by what you say of my book"—he went on to defend himself:

Your gentleness too makes me stop and think. Perhaps you are right in your adverse view of my sometimes obstreperous objections to decorum. I must think more of that. But each must free himself from the bonds of banality as best he can; you or another may turn into a lively field of intelligent activity quite easily but I being perhaps more timid or unstable at heart, must free myself by more violent methods. I cannot object to rhetoric, as you point out, but I must object to the academic associations with which rhetoric is hung and which vitiate all its significance by making the piece of work to which it is applied a dried bone. And so I have made the mistake of abusing the very thing I most use.[25]

Williams is responding to Moore's contention that "despite Dr. Williams' championing of the school of ignorance, or rather of no school but experience, there is in his work the authoritativeness, the wise silence which knows schools and fashions. . . ."[26] Alluding to Williams' prologue to *Kora in Hell*, where he combatively takes on Pound, H.D., Stevens, and Eliot, Moore suggests that Williams does not take criticism well from those who wish to offer advice about how he might improve his work:

But one who sets out to appraise him has temerity, since he speaks derisively of the wish of certain of his best friends to improve his work and, after all, the conflict between the tendency to aesthetic anarchy and the necessity for self imposed discipline must take care of itself.[27]

For Moore this early conflict in Williams never did resolve itself. Initially, however, she believed that Williams would correct or modify his rebellious tendencies. This hope may have made Moore more open about expressing her reservations in this first review than she would be in subsequent reviews of his work.

At this stage Moore could acknowledge Williams' desire to stand alone—"his passion for being himself"[28]—and connect him with confidence to other writers she admired:

The acknowledgment of our debt to the imagination, constitutes, perhaps, his positive value. Compression, colour, speed, accuracy and that restraint of instinctive craftsmanship which precludes anything dowdy or laboured—it is essentially these qualities that we have in his work. Burke speaks of the imagination as the most intensive province of pleasure and pain and defines it as a creative power of the mind, representing at pleasure the images of things in the order and manner in which they were received by the senses or in combining them in a new manner and according to a different order. Dr. Williams in his power over the actual, corroborates this statement. Observe how, by means of his rehabilitating power of the mind, he is able to fix the atmosphere of a moment:

"It is still warm enough to slip from the woods into the lake's edge . . . and snake's eggs lie curling in the sun on the lonely summit."[29]

Moore had praised Williams' use of compression as early as 1917. "Your compression," she had written, "makes me feel that the Japanese haven't the field to themselves."[30] Later in the review she comes back to a consideration of Williams' speed, maintaining that even when we cannot follow him, we are aware of his work's "crisp exterior":

> The sharpened faculties which require exactness, instant satisfaction and an underpinning of truth are too abrupt in their activities sometimes to follow; but the niceness and effect of vigor for which they are responsible, are never absent from Dr. Williams' work and its crisp exterior is one of its great distinctions.[31]

In addition to praising qualities of Williams' technique, Moore shows how Williams' work supports Edmund Burke's ideas about the imagination. Burke, she maintains, recognizes the double function of the imagination; the imagination can represent things in the order in which they are perceived or can combine them in a completely new order. Moore then yokes together two separate quotations from Williams to illustrate how Williams' transforming imagination supports Burke's assertions. "It is still warm enough to slip from the woods into the lake's edge . . . and snake's eggs lie curling in the sun on the lonely summit."

Moore also likens Williams to Sir Francis Bacon in that both have the ability to see similarities between things which are different from one another:

> "By the brokenness of his composition," he writes, "the poet makes himself master of a certain weapon which he could possess himself of in no other way." We do not so much feel the force of this statement as we feel that there is in life, as there is in Sir Francis Bacon—in the ability to see resemblances in things which are dissimilar; in the ability to see such differences, a special kind of imagination is required, which Dr. Williams has.[32]

Despite Williams' particular type of imagination, Moore also praises him for knowing how to survive without this faculty "in

the direst poverty of the imagination."[33] Sandwiched between
two statements about Williams' desire to divorce himself from
"schools and fashions," Moore lists four quotations from *Kora in
Hell*; her improvisation serves to reconcile certain oppositions in
Williams' aesthetic between art (or the imagination) and nature
(or the material realm). Moore's arrangement of these quotations
is her own; the quotations do not appear in this order in *Kora
in Hell*:

> "Lamps carry far, believe me," he says, "in lieu of sunshine."
> "What can it mean to you that a child wears pretty clothes
> and speaks three languages or that its mother goes to the best
> shops? . . . Men . . . buy finery and indulge in extravagant
> moods in order to piece out their lack with other matter."
> "Kindly stupid hands, kindly coarse voices, . . . infinitely
> detached, infinitely beside the question . . . and night is done
> and the green edge of yesterday has said all it could."
> "In middle life the mind passes to a variegated October.
> This is the time youth in its faulty aspirations has set for the
> achievement of great summits. But having attained the moun-
> tain top one is not snatched into a cloud but the descent prof-
> fers its blandishments quite as a matter of course. At this the
> fellow is cast into a great confusion and rather plaintively looks
> about to see if any has fared better than he."[34]

By defining Williams' aesthetic as one that depends on the ex-
istence of opposing forces, Moore anticipates Stevens' argument
in his preface to Williams' *Collected Poems*. Artificial light (lamps)
can compensate for or transform the absence of natural light
(sunshine). One indulges in "matter" in the absence of the imagi-
nation; notice what Moore's ellipsis conceals in her second quo-
tation: "But men in the direst poverty of the imagination buy
finery and indulge in extravagant moods in order to piece out
their lack with other matter." We are also asked to accept that
"the green edge of yesterday has said all it could." And finally, to

attain "the mountain top" is to recognize that the descent offers its own benefits. Moore increasingly came to feel that Williams abandoned this aesthetic; and in 1951 when Book Four of *Paterson* was published she was convinced of this.

Between 1921 when she reviewed *Kora in Hell* and 1926 when Williams received the *Dial* Award, Moore did not review Williams' other work. Although she did write an anonymous "Briefer Mention" of Williams' *In the American Grain* for *The Dial* in 1926, this did not constitute a full-length review. Moore did not hesitate to criticize Williams in this short statement: "Unsubmissive to his pessimism and sometimes shocked by the short work which he makes of decorum, verbal and other, we wisely salute the here assembled phosphorescent findings of a search prosecuted 'with antennae extended.'"[35] Moore seems to have written this "Briefer Mention" because she and Watson could not find anyone else who was willing to do a longer review.[36] Between 1921 and 1926 Williams published several works that Moore might have reviewed, but chose not to: *Sour Grapes* (1921), *Spring and All* (1923), and *The Great American Novel* (1923). When Williams received the 1926 *Dial* Award, Moore, who was editor of *The Dial* at this time, wrote the announcement confirming the award.

This announcement then constitutes her second review of his work, though this time she does not focus on one text. Moore is no longer directly critical of Williams' defiant posture, but her tone and method reveal an ambivalence that is not immediately apparent. Often she detaches herself by quoting other people on Williams. In one instance, she applies something Williams said about Poe to Williams himself: "His 'venomous accuracy,' if we may use the words used by him in speaking of the author of The Raven, is opposed to 'makeshifts, self-deceptions and grotesque excuses.'"[37] She also quotes an unnamed "connoisseur of our poetry" who is reputed to have compared Williams to Chekhov: "'This modest quality of realness which he attributes to 'contact'

with the good Jersey dirt sometimes reminds one of Chekhov,'
says a connoisseur of our poetry. 'Like Chekhov he knows ani-
mals and babies as well as trees. And to people who are looking
for the story his poems must often seem as disconnected and cen-
trifugal as Chekhov's later plays.'"[38] Moore also quotes William
Marion Reedy:

> He [Williams] "is forthright, a hard, straight, bitter javelin,"
> said William Marion Reedy. "As you read him you catch in
> your nostrils the pungent beauty in the wake of his 'hard stuff,'
> and you begin to realize how little poetry—or prose—depends
> on definitions, or precedents, or forms." You do.[39]

Moore's barely noticeable comment—"You do"—allows her to
assert her own presence tentatively without giving up her studied
neutrality.

Toward the end of the announcement Moore sets up an anal-
ogy between Williams and Sir Thomas Browne:

> We have said that Carlos Williams is a doctor. Physicians are
> not so often poets as poets are physicians, but may we not as-
> sert confidently that oppositions of science are not oppositions
> to poetry but oppositions to falseness. The author of the Religio
> Medici could not be called anything more than he could be
> called a poet. "He has many verba ardentia," as Samuel John-
> son has observed—"forcible expressions, which he would
> never have found, but by venturing to the utmost verge of pro-
> priety; and flights which would never have been reached, but
> by one who had very little fear of the shame of falling."[40]

As Moore quotes Samuel Johnson on Sir Thomas Browne, she
drops out of sight, avoiding in the process a direct critique of
Williams. We are invited, however, to see an implicit connection
between Browne's forceful expressions and Williams' "'venom-
ous accuracy'"; Williams, we infer, has also ventured to the very

edge of propriety, and like Browne, is not afraid of going too far in his "flights."

Moore's method of quoting other people's judgments in this review instead of merely offering her own serves to distance her from the subject at hand—Williams' poetry and prose up to this point—and to conceal her ambivalence about this subject. This is most apparent when she quotes Wallace Stevens. After a lengthy catalogue of Williams' subject matter—"fences and outhouses built of barrel-staves and parts of boxes," "The Passaic, that filthy river," "hawsers that drop and groan," and "a young horse with a green bed-quilt on his withers"—Moore remarks: "We need not, as Wallace Stevens has said, 'try to . . . evolve a mainland from his [Williams'] leaves, scents and floating bottles and boxes.' 'What Columbus discovered is nothing to what Williams is looking for.'"[41]

This critical alliance with Stevens is worth examining. Moore seems to suggest here that Stevens would advise us not to seek some overall unity in Williams because Williams himself, unlike Columbus, was not looking for this. In fact, Stevens had said just the opposite in the private letter to her that Moore quotes publicly in the *Dial* announcement. Some time in 1925 Moore had apparently written to Stevens from *The Dial*, soliciting a review of Williams' *In the American Grain*, for Stevens wrote to her on November 19, 1925:

> And I feel sure that one of the things I ought not to do is to review Williams' book. What Columbus discovered is nothing to what Williams is looking for. However much I might like to try to make that out—evolve a mainland from his leaves, scents and floating bottles and boxes—there is a baby at home.[42]

Stevens does not say here, as Moore says he does in her review, that one need not try to find out what Williams is searching for; rather he says that if he were to attempt to discover what Williams is after he would have to make something coherent out of his subject matter. Moore misrepresents Stevens in order to justify her own reticence about approaching Williams; her identification with Stevens' private admission sanctions her own public need not to figure out what Williams is seeking, the implication being that the search might be in vain.

Moore continued to want Stevens to write something for *The Dial* about Williams. We can assume that she wrote to him again after her 1925 request for a review of *In the American Grain* because Stevens wrote to Moore on December 3, 1926:

> I am incessantly and atrociously busy—else I should like more than I can say to act as midwife for Williams' spirit. I have not the time. I don't say that I could bring the burden forth: merely that I have not the time to try.[43]

Once again Stevens expresses reservations about his ability to launch Williams.

Moore's interest in Stevens' aesthetic made her eager to see what he would, or could, do with Williams.[44] Thus when she reviewed Williams' *Collected Poems* in 1934 Moore framed and concluded her own discussion with references to Stevens' preface.[45] She gives Stevens' preface a prominent place in her own review for several reasons. Stevens articulates ideas about Williams' aesthetic that Moore had addressed, in a less expository fashion, when she reviewed *Kora in Hell* in 1921. In addition, for her prefaces and introductions become part of the text and must be contended with. Also, by paying homage to Stevens' preface Moore could conceal her own ambivalence about Williams, or at least shield herself from immediate detection by hiding behind the mask Stevens' preface provided.

Williams had asked Stevens to write the preface. Later, however, in *I Wanted to Write a Poem*, he reacted with displeasure to it:

I was pleased when Wallace Stevens agreed to write the Preface but nettled when I read the part where he said I was interested in the anti-poetic. I had never thought consciously of such a thing. As a poet I was using a means of getting an effect. It's all one to me—the anti-poetic is not something to enhance the poetic—it's all one piece. I didn't agree with Stevens that it was a conscious means I was using. I have never been satisfied that the anti-poetic had any validity or even existed.[46]

Williams' contention here that the anti-poetic neither enhances the poetic nor is separate from it is a public version of his early private arguments with Moore about "the lily and the mud"— "one as 'lovely' technically speaking, as the other!"

Williams would have been even more displeased with Stevens' preface if he had seen a letter Stevens wrote to T. C. Wilson in March of 1935:

. . . it would suit me very well to go over [Moore's] poems, because I think what she does is really a good deal more important than what Williams does. I cannot help feeling that Williams represents a somewhat exhausted phase of the romantic. . . .[47]

Stevens begins his preface by identifying Williams as "a romantic poet." But, he maintains, he "is rarely romantic in the accepted sense. . . . The man has spent his life in rejecting the accepted sense of things." Williams, Stevens argues, is a romantic because "he has a sentimental side." But he is not merely sentimental; he combines "a little sentiment, very little, together with acute reaction." Williams' aesthetic, according to Stevens, involves "a passion for the anti-poetic."[48] Yet Stevens contends: "Something of the unreal is necessary to fecundate the real; something of the sentimental is necessary to fecundate the anti-poetic." Thus, for Stevens, Williams' poetry grows out of "the constant interaction of two opposites." Finally, for Stevens a romantic poet is one who "dwells in an ivory tower, but who insists that life would be intolerable except for the fact that one has, from the top, such an exceptional view of the public dump and the advertising signs of Snider's Catsup, Ivory Soap and Chevrolet Cars. . . ."[49]

Like Stevens, Moore points in her review of *Collected Poems* to Williams' sentimental side, and like Stevens she sees this sentiment tempered by what Stevens calls "acute reaction." Williams, Moore observes, can be "sorry for the tethered bull, the circus sea-elephant, for the organ-grinder 'sourfaced,' for the dead man 'needing a shave,'"[50] but she reminds us "the pathos is incidental. The 'ability to be drunk with a sudden realization of value in things others never notice' can metamorphose our detestable reasonableness and offset a whole planetary system of deadness."[51] Moore's remarks were in keeping with her 1927 *Dial* essay, "A Poet of the Quattrocento," in which she had also praised Williams for his ability to transform the quotidian, for "his manner of contemplating with new eyes, old things, shabby things, and other things. . . ."[52]

Moore ends her review with a reference to the importance of prose from a poet like Stevens:

> Dr. Williams does not compromise, and Wallace Stevens is another resister whose way of saying is as important as what is said. Mr. Stevens' presentation of the book refreshes a grievance—the scarcity of prose about verse from one of the few persons who should have something to say. But poetry in America has not died, so long as these two "young sycamores" are able to stand the winters that we have, and the inhabitants.[53]

Moore is undoubtedly referring here to Stevens' refusal to contribute prose—particularly about Williams—to *The Dial*. Yet despite her quarrel with Williams, at the end of her review Moore unites Stevens and Williams—"these two 'young sycamores'"—

in the same enterprise; they must contend with the inhospitable climate in which they produce their poetry and the unreceptive public who receives it.

While Moore certainly agreed for the most part with Stevens' reading of Williams, it was not the only reading of Williams she would endorse in 1934. Although she frames and concludes her review with references to Stevens' preface, some of her judgments of Williams differ from those of Stevens. For example, Stevens finds that Williams "is commonly identified by externals" such as "abortive rhythms, words on several levels, ideas without logic, and similar minor matters," but he concludes that "when all is said," these "are merely the diversion of the prophet between morning and evening song."[54] Moore does not share Stevens' reservations about Williams' technique. In fact it is one of the things she praises in this review:

> Disliking the tawdriness of unnecessary explanation, the de-tracting compulsory connective, stock speech of any kind, he sets the words down, "each note secure in its own posture— singularly woven." "The senseless unarrangement of wild things" which he imitates makes some kinds of correct writing look rather foolish. . . .[55]

These were the same values Williams had identified and cham-pioned in Moore's work in 1925.

Moore differs from Stevens' assumptions in still another re-gard. Stevens situates Williams, like other romantic poets, "in an ivory tower," gazing from afar at "the public dump." In his essay "Stevens and Williams: The Epistemology of Modernism," Albert Gelpi points out that Stevens describes himself here rather than Williams:

> The problem with Stevens' description of the romantic as ideal-istic solipsist in a shabby, commercialized society is that it befits him more than Williams. It is Stevens who would write "The

Man on the Dump" from an ivory tower elevation that per-
mitted the exotic figurations and highfalutin language of that
poem. Williams, never as reclusive as Stevens, would choose to
squat on the dump, reading the rotten Paterson or Rutherford
newspaper.[56]

Moore, who agreed with Stevens concerning the necessity of cul-
tivating a distance, had felt for a long time that Williams flirted a
bit too much with the dump. Now, in 1934, she was convinced of
this: "His uncompromising conscientiousness sometimes seems
misplaced; he is at times almost insultingly unevasive. . . ."[57] For
Moore this tendency was another example of what she had re-
ferred to in 1921 as Williams' "aesthetic anarchy." Although she
recognized the perils of excessive evasiveness in writers as differ-
ent as Stevens and Pound, Moore also knew the danger Williams
ran by not being evasive enough. Not surprisingly, in the letters
she wrote to Williams after 1934, Moore brought up this issue
again.

Moore did not write about Williams publicly again until 1936.
She did, however, continue to react privately to his work. When
Ronald Lane Latimer, who was at the Alcestis Press, published
Williams' *An Early Martyr* in 1935, Moore wrote to him:

You and Dr. Williams are surely to be congratulated on
the title of this book—AN EARLY MARTYR. William Carlos
Williams in himself is one who makes one not ashamed of
being an American. I wish in his desperation against the un-
changeable and the abominable he need not come so near
running his thrust. There is nothing like it when it comes
straight.[58]

A longer letter Moore wrote to Williams about the book ten
days later sheds considerable light on what she had meant when
she called attention to Williams' tendencies to be combative:

You are doing here what you seem to think Gertrude Stein is doing, in making words live. ITEM is for me one of the most consoling and eloquent things in existence; impressive indeed as springing not from the splinters of battle but from the heat of the mind. THE LOCUST TREE IN FLOWER is the complete manual of poetics, (the delicacy of the added article in itself is indicative); FLOWERS BY THE SEA, a very strange apex on one of the things you have always done best. The title, AN EARLY MARTYR; perfection—with a note in it of the whole thing. I could go on this way, of every one; *nearly* [Moore's emphasis] every one; for there are some I shall never understand; nor why it is necessary you should do a certain thing. One's compulsions are tyrants; one suffers for them. D. H. Lawrence certainly did and one cannot have contempt for him. I should say it is easier to avoid the ignoble public than to punish it. And I cannot get rid, in such outrages of conscience, of the fact of myself. I do not care to become a polecat in order to make polecats admit they are that, and confess their injuriousness. I cannot see that art is in any way different from the rest of life, from conversation or from the strategies of solitude; and it is an unending query with me why a person would say on the page what he has never been known to say to your face. I hope you won't dislike me too much for saying to your face what I don't say on the page.[59]

Moore, who a year earlier had begun her review of Williams' *Collected Poems* by maintaining that "struggle . . . is a main force in William Carlos Williams," now contends that Williams' poem "Item" is impressive because it is a product of reflection and not of struggle. She now praises Williams for his distance from the battle. Moore attempts to place Williams back in Stevens' ivory tower, implicitly advising him to maintain "his exceptional view of the public dump." But this is only part of what she writes to

Williams about his current enterprise; the praise of the first part of the letter must be seen in the context of what follows. For Moore, all too often Williams still does write "from the splinters of battle," and in these moments he loses his necessary perspective and his compulsions become tyrants. Moore hints that Williams ought to ignore the base public, as she does, rather than try to chastise it. She advocates that Williams adopt a mask, instead of insisting on becoming "a polecat in order to make polecats admit they are that."

When Williams received Moore's letter he wrote back immediately:

> I'm glad you have the book and that you liked it well enough to speak freely about it. I thoroughly sympathize with your position. But to me a book is somewhat of a confessional. It is just because I do not say things—that—I would—say that I must write them. It would not be fair to a reader for me to hold back knowledge of the matrix from which comes the possible gem.
>
> It goes further than that with me. There is a good deal of rebellion still in what I write, rebellion against stereotype poetic process—the too miraculous choice among other things. In too much refinement there lurks a sterility that wishes to pass too often for purity when it is anything but that. Coarseness for its own sake is inexcusable but a Rabelaisian sanity requires that the rare and the fine be exhibited as coming like everything else from the dirt. There is no incompatibility between them.[60]

Williams, unlike Moore, does not see any need to cultivate a mask or to keep his distance from the public. Rather than residing in an ivory tower, Williams maintains that for him writing is a kind of intimate confession—the origins of which must be shared with his reader. He denies the validity of Stevens' dichotomy between the anti-poetic and the poetic and reactivates his old argument with Moore about "the lily and the mud." The tone of Williams' response was certainly familiar to Moore, for this was hardly the first time he had written to her about his need to rebel against "stereotype poetic process."

In 1936 Moore wrote her last review of Williams; she reviewed *Adam & Eve & the City* for the *Brooklyn Daily Eagle*. This time Moore could privately applaud Williams' efforts, though she was less specific about what she admired in this volume than she had been previously about what she disliked in a given collection. In a letter to Williams in December of 1936, Moore wrote:

> I cannot so much as touch on *Adam & Eve & the City*; it sets me off toward so much that needs italics. In some ways it is your hardest and finest product and as I said to Ezra P. last month on hearing from him for the first time in a year or so, what a wonderful thing it is to augment as you (W.C. Williams) do, rather than parch.[61]

When reviewing Williams' *Adam & Eve & the City* later that month, Moore again quotes Stevens, but this time her critical alliance does not serve to mask her own uneasiness with Williams. Without hiding behind Stevens, she openly challenges Williams: "As Wallace Stevens says, 'poets are never of the world in which they live.' But does Dr. Williams realize—would he admit, one wonders—that every one is an exile?" Backing off a bit from the implications of her rhetorical question, she asserts: "Possibly; for he is honest, prompt to submit his premise, serious to the point of bitterness, compassionate; ruled by affection and the compulsion to usefulness."[62] Perhaps Moore is accusing Williams of trying to immerse himself in *this* world in a way that she and Stevens insisted was both impossible and unproductive; or she may be alluding to Williams' desire to be part of some "community"—another impulse which Moore and Stevens would undoubtedly have rejected for themselves.

In any case, shortly after the review appeared, Williams responded to Moore's charge that they were all "exiles":

> If only—I keep saying year in year out—it were possible for "us" to have a place, a location, to which we could resort, singly or otherwise, and to which others could follow us as dogs follow each other—without formality but surely—where we could be known as poets and our work be seen—and we could see the work of others and buy it and have it! Why can't such a thing come about? It seems so brainless and spineless a thing for us to be "exiles" in too literal and accepted a sense. Being exiles might we not at least, as exiles, consort more easily together? We seem needlessly isolated and we suffer dully, supinely. I am not one for leading a crusade, but I'd lead a little group through the underbrush to a place in the woods, or under a barn if I thought anyone would (or perhaps, could) follow me. Or I'd follow.[63]

Williams ignores the implications of Moore's assertion "that every one is an exile." He also does not respond to her quotation from Stevens: "Poets are never of the world in which they live." For a poet who advocated an aesthetic of immersion in the people and things around him, his response is markedly elitist. Courting the privileges of withdrawing from the public, Williams appears to welcome such an exodus if he can be a part of some select group of poets.

Moore wrote back immediately; her response indicated that they had reached an impasse. "If there were 'a little group' consorting ('in a barn, 'in the woods' or other place) I would not be there. . . ."[64] Moore did not go on to elaborate on their differences, as she had in some of her earlier letters.

She did, however, still have reservations about his work. Earlier that year, Williams had introduced Moore to Mary Barnard, one of the many poets he was trying to launch. Mariani describes their meeting:

The following Friday evening, Mary Barnard went to "Farru-
gio's apartment" at 62 Montague Street in Brooklyn Heights
(overlooking lower Manhattan) for a party thrown by Ronald
Lane Latimer. There she met Marianne Moore, the critic Ruth
Lechlitner, Latimer, and saw Williams again. It was the first
time Williams himself had seen Marianne Moore in several
years and Barnard found that Moore kept up an incessant bar-
rage of words because—as Williams told Barnard later—she
"was frightened and was trying to build up a barrier of words
to hide behind." Moore left early and Williams withdrew to
sign the colophon sheets for *Adam & Eve & the City.* Interest-
ingly, Moore had advised Barnard "not to pay any attention to
what Dr. Williams told [her]—as to content. As for technical
advice, he might be very good." [65]

When she reviewed *Adam & Eve & the City* later that year,
Moore avoided discussing Williams' content. Instead she focused
almost exclusively on his technical accomplishments. Keeping
her earlier objections at a distance—"temperament does not
change and Dr. Williams is not becoming sociological, hostile to
war or vivid against injustice; he was always all of these. But
he does seem, with time, wiser and juster; and more completely
the poet" [66]—Moore praises Williams' "end rhymes and inner
rhymes," and she contends: "The welded ease of his composi-
tions resembles the linked self-propelled momentum of sprocket
and chain. . . ." She also identifies his "respect for rhythm as per-
sonality" in "his unwillingness to substitute meter of his own for
the rocking-horse rhythm of the Lupercio de Argensola poems
translated by him here. . . ." [67]

Moore is protective of Williams in her review. In her conversa-
tion notebook for December of 1936, we find the following:

W.C. Williams There was no sale at first for
    Anthracite coal People did not know how to use it
    + wanted bituminous [Moore's emphasis]

> W.C. Williams, think of him, forgive him, help
> him—[68]

Drawing directly on the first of these notes, she concludes her review by suggesting that with time people will come to appreciate what Williams is doing:

> Anthracite coal did not sell at first; people wanted bituminous, and had to learn with time that anthracite is cleaner and burns longer. In the same way, Dr. Williams is substituting good fuel for the more transitory.[69]

Despite Moore's almost wholly positive public reception of *Adam & Eve & the City*, in retrospect her reaction to *Paterson* in 1951 could have been predicted. For Moore the gap between the aesthetic Williams defined in *Kora in Hell* and *Spring and All* and the poetry he subsequently produced only widened. Over the years she became increasingly uncomfortable with what Williams chose to write about even though she continued to admire his technique. "Some of your 'everyday' images," she wrote to him in 1941, "I would say are too everyday to be condoned. . . . Internal poison may require external poison to counteract it but there certainly must be a point at which the dose becomes dangerous."[70] Publicly in her reviews, however, Moore avoided this issue altogether or disguised her ambivalence about it. Yet in her letters to Williams, particularly after 1934, Moore made no attempt to hide her criticism of his work.

Like Moore, Stevens also found Williams' everyday images increasingly difficult to tolerate. In a letter to José Rodríguez Feo in December of 1946, he confided:

> And, of course, Williams is an old friend of mine. I have not read Paterson. I have the greatest respect for him, although there is the constant difficulty that he is more interested in the way of saying things than in what he has to say. The fact remains that we are always fundamentally interested in what a

writer has to say. When we are sure of that, we pay attention to the way in which he says it, not often before.[71]

While Moore could still admire Williams' technique, Stevens refused to separate what Williams wrote about from the way he approached his subject matter. In short, Stevens could no longer pretend to accept Williams' aesthetic of "no ideas but in things." In her private exchanges with Williams, Moore continued to let him know that she found his refusal to transform his world unacceptable.

5 "Combative sincerity" and "Studious constraint": The Literary Exchanges of Moore and Eliot

... the public thirst for words about poetry, and for words from poets about almost anything—in contrast to its thirst for poetry itself—seems insatiable.[1]

Some day or other when the labours of both of us have ceased, there will, I trust, be a nice little volume for Faber & Faber of "Letters from Marianne Moore to T. S. Eliot."[2]

On September 6, 1935, Moore sent T. S. Eliot a cheque in the amount of fifteen dollars in an effort to share the royalties she had recently received from Faber and Faber for sales from her *Selected Poems* (1935). Eliot was reluctant to accept this curious and unexpected donation from Moore and wrote back: "You are one of the strangest children I have ever had anything to do with. Why should you send me a cheque for 15 dollars?"[3] Moore took notice of Eliot's reference to her as a child and responded:

You are a strange *parent* [Moore's emphasis] to be willing to disfurnish me in this way of a pleasure. I had had some thought of asking Mr. Stewart or whoever it is that administers the Faber & Faber authors' finances, to execute my decision impersonally as it were, and transfer to you the two pounds, seventeen shillings and pence. You do not seem to realize that the book would not be a book or source of money to anyone, had my judgment about it prevailed.[4]

The alacrity with which Moore appropriates Eliot's terms, becoming the rebellious child and casting Eliot in the role of the discerning parent, is telling for what it reveals about the tone of their relationship during the thirties. Their early exchanges also prepare us for this dynamic of strange child and strange parent.

For some time Eliot had taken a parental role concerning the publishing of Moore's work. As early as 1921 he had offered to try to get a book of her poems published.[5] Moore was clearly pleased with his offer. "Were I to publish verse," she wrote back, "I should be grateful indeed for the assistance you offer." But she added, "For me to be published so would merely emphasize the meagerness of my production." Finally, Moore seemed more pleased with Eliot's desire to promote her than she did with the possibility of the book itself: "But to have friends," she concluded, "is the great thing. I value more than I am able to say, your approval."[6] What is essential here is that Moore valued Eliot's approval because she valued his critical sensibility. The critic in her scheme is cast in the role of a parent who may or may not approve of an artist's or child's work. For Moore, the critic is not merely "someone who comes late"[7] to the text, but someone whose presence makes the text possible.

Later in 1921 when Bryher and H.D. published Moore's *Poems* with Egoist Press, Moore was quick to inform Eliot of this:

> Since you were so kind as to propose the collecting and publishing of work of mine, I wish to send you a copy of the book which Miss Bryher has brought out—Its publication was a tremendous surprise to me—[8]

Then, instead of commenting on Eliot's by then well-launched poetic enterprise, Moore added: "Allow me to wish you all possible good in the completion of your analyses of poetry."[9] This

became a pattern in their correspondence: Eliot would write
to Moore about her poetry and she would write to him primarily
about his criticism.

In May of 1925, for example, Moore wrote to Eliot that she
was glad that he was pleased to have received the *Dial* Award.
Without even mentioning *The Waste Land*—the poem that was re-
sponsible for his receiving the award—she proceeded to praise
Eliot's *Homage to John Dryden* for being "rich in entertainment
and analysis. . . ." "I venture to hope," Moore continued, "that
you will yet write criticisms upon other poets of the 17th and 18th
centuries." [10] Moore's public and private silence on the subject of
The Waste Land becomes a strange presence as one reads through
their correspondence. In fact, in March of 1934, we find one of
the few references to *The Waste Land* in one of Moore's letters to
Eliot. "I am sometimes asked," she wrote to him on March 15,
1934, "if I would like to make a great deal of money by selling
my Boni & Liveright Dial Award copy of THE WASTE LAND—a
query that led me to think you ought to have any copies that
could be secured." [11] Although Moore, like others, recognized
the monetary value of Eliot's poem, she obviously had no am-
bivalence about parting with her Boni and Liveright *Dial*
Award copy.

We also find that she made no notes in the back of her copies
of Eliot's poetry, while in her copies of his criticism and his plays
there are copious notes.[12] As I documented in chapter 3, Moore
followed Eliot's criticism of Pound particularly closely. In June of
1934, shortly after she reviewed Pound's *Cantos* for *The Criterion*,
Moore wrote to Eliot, thanking him for sending her a copy of
Pound's *Selected Poems*: "I have received the Pound *Selected Poems*
and am much interested in your carefully unequivocal analysis
and in the choice of poems. I wish I had had this by me when
writing on the Cantos." [13] What Moore does not mention to Eliot
is the criticism of his which she had consulted when writing on
Pound's *Cantos* for the first time in 1931.[14] Still following Eliot's

criticism of Pound with avid interest, Moore wrote to him on November 4, 1946, praising his essay on Pound that had appeared in *Poetry* that year.

> If anything could strike the shackles from Ezra Pound, it would certainly be your account of him in *Poetry*—which being (like the Faber and Faber catalogues) exact and yet free, liberates others of us along with him.[15]

Eliot was certainly interested in Moore's reviews of her contemporaries; he solicited for *The Criterion* both her 1934 review of Pound's *Cantos* and a review of Williams' *Collected Poems*. Moore declined to review Williams again, having just reviewed his *Collected Poems* for *Poetry*. She had reviewed Pound's *Draft of XXX Cantos* once before as well, in 1931 for *Poetry*, but was pleased to have the opportunity to write about his project again.[16] Yet although Eliot asked Moore for reviews for *The Criterion*, he was more consistently enthusiastic about her poetry and the possibility of promoting it.[17] Eliot never offered, for example, to publish a collection of Moore's essays, though he did mention to her in 1956 that he was interested in having Faber and Faber publish a collection of her letters to him.[18]

Eliot's promotion of Moore's poetic enterprise was a major one. In 1923 he again broached the subject of sponsoring her work. On October 4, 1923, he wrote to her, telling her he had just sent an article about her poetry to *The Dial*. He also reiterated his earlier offer to publish a collection of her poetry: "When you are ready to publish another book here let me know." Thinking per haps of the lack of attention Moore's *Poems* (1921) had received, Eliot maintained, "I think I could 'float' it better than the last which never got a fair show."[19]

Moore was delighted with an essay by Eliot that appeared in the 1923 December issue of *The Dial*. Eliot singled out her "quite new rhythm," her "brilliant and rather satirical use of . . . simply the curious jargon produced in America by universal university education," and her "almost primitive simplicity of phrase."[20] Citing Moore's "Those Various Scalpels," Eliot asserted: "Here the rhythm depends partly upon the transformation-changes from one image to another, so that the second image is superposed before the first has quite faded, and upon the dexterity of change of vocabulary from one image to another."[21]

A brief quotation from "Those Various Scalpels" will serve to illustrate Eliot's analysis:

> your eyes, flowers of ice and snow
>
> sown by tearing winds on the cordage of disabled ships; your
>   raised hand,
>   an ambiguous signature: your cheeks, those rosettes
>   of blood on the stone floors of French châteaux,
>   with regard to which the guides are so affirmative—

Moore's "anthology of transit" here (Williams used this phrase in 1925 to describe her poem "Marriage") forces our eyes to move from one image to another before we have fully assimilated the first one.[22] In his introduction to her *Selected Poems* Eliot would return to the difficulty of following "so alert an eye": "The bewilderment consequent upon trying to follow so alert an eye, so quick a process of association, may produce the effect of some 'metaphysical' poetry."[23]

When Moore read Eliot's essay she wrote to him, indicating that she especially appreciated his treatment of her rhythm, "that pleasantry of speech which characterizes the American language," and "what you say of simplicity of phrase."[24] As if her own praise were not sufficient, Moore added: "Charles Demuth spoke to me recently of the skill in the very perfect finish of your writing in this article. . . ."[25]

Given Eliot's incisive reading of Moore's early poems, it is not surprising that Eliot was the one person she most wanted to write the introduction for her *Selected Poems* in 1935. In June of 1935

Moore confided to Eliot: "You will be amused to note—whereas I am profoundly grateful for—the armor afforded me by your introduction to my book." [26] A brief examination of Eliot's introduction will demonstrate why Moore felt protected by this preface and pleased with the insights Eliot offered the public—insights which in most instances complemented those he had explored in his 1923 review of her work.

After expressing a healthy skepticism about the critic's role in assessing his contemporaries, Eliot pokes fun at the masses: "One of the tests—though it be only a negative test—of anything really new and genuine, seems to be its capacity for exciting aversion among 'lovers of poetry.' " [27] Moore loved the tone of this observation. Writing to Eliot on October 23, 1934, she maintained:

> A test "of anything really new and genuine, seems to be its capacity for exciting aversion among 'lovers of poetry' " is one of your tallest strokes and "if you aim only at the poetry in poetry there is no poetry either" is another.[28]

Eliot's assertions throughout the introduction were calculated, in Moore's eyes, to undermine a public reception that might be other than positive. "I cannot speak fitly—in fact at all," Moore wrote in her letter of October 23, "of the coolness with which you spike the guns of the critic before he attacks. . . . Unless I compel myself however to have done with my appreciations, you will feel that authors are more dangerous than the public." [29]

In his introduction to her *Selected Poems*, Eliot effectively deals with Moore's dangerous public. But he is not merely dismissive of a community of bad, unreceptive readers. His brilliant analysis of what Moore is after sets the tone for most of the criticism of Moore which follows in the thirties, forties, and fifties.[30] Given Eliot's prominent position in the critical community, no assessments of Moore's poetry could fail to consider and acknowledge, if only implicitly, his reading.

One of Eliot's most perceptive insights was to stress the use of "minute detail" in Moore's poetry over "that of emotional unity."[31] In the following passage Eliot defines the epistemological implications of Moore's poetic:

> The gift for detailed observation, for finding the exact words for some experience of the eye, is liable to disperse the attention of the relaxed reader. The minutiae may even irritate the unwary, or arouse in them only the pleasurable astonishment evoked by the carved ivory ball with eleven other balls inside it . . . The bewilderment consequent upon trying to follow so alert an eye, so quick a process of association, may produce the effect of some "metaphysical" poetry. . . . But the detail has always its service to perform to the whole. The similes are there for use; as the mussel-shell "opening and shutting itself like an injured fan" (where *injured* has an ambiguity good enough for Mr. Empson), the waves "as formal as the scales on a fish." They make us see the object more clearly, though we may not understand immediately why our attention has been called to this object . . . she succeeds at once in startling us into an unusual awareness of visual patterns, with something like the fascination of a high-powered microscope.[32]

Eliot's metaphor of a high-powered microscope is apt, for Moore repeatedly asks us to look at the part, the detail, the minutiae, closely and intensely, before allowing us to approximate its relationship to the whole. Her way of connecting the objects in her world calls into question the possibility of seeing the whole without first seeing the fragments of which it consists. Finally, Moore breaks down traditional boundaries between the object itself and our ways of appropriating knowledge about it.

Eliot is also particularly sensitive to the temperament behind these poems and the need to protect that temperament from those who want explanations about "our most powerful and most secret release":

> Some of Miss Moore's poems—for instance with animal or bird subjects—have a very wide spread of association. It would be difficult to say what is the "subject-matter" of "The Jerboa." For a mind of such agility, and for a sensibility so reticent, the minor subject, such as a pleasant little sand-coloured skipping animal, may be the best release for the major emotions. Only the pedantic literalist could consider the subject-matter to be trivial; the triviality is in himself. We all have to choose whatever subject-matter allows us the most powerful and most secret release; and that is a personal affair.[33]

Moore's choice of subjects, Eliot suggests, complements both the agility of her mind and her reticent sensibility. Here, I suspect, Eliot implicitly defends his own reticence and choice of subject matter in his poems.

I now turn to the private exchange between Moore and Eliot which led up to Eliot's writing this introduction for Moore's *Selected Poems*, for her dependency on Eliot—her "strange parent"—has much to do with the enormous role he played in publishing this collection of her poetry. In January of 1934 Eliot wrote to Moore from Faber and Faber: "I have thought for some time that your poems ought to be collected, or at any rate selected, and put upon the London market again."[34] Eliot had an uncanny sense of timing; at a time when Moore's American publisher, Macmillan, had not yet considered publishing a volume of her selected poems, Eliot seized the moment and began negotiations to have Faber and Faber publish her *Selected Poems*. Moore's *Poems*, her first volume, was no longer readily available and *Observations*, though published in two editions, one in 1924 and one in 1925, had little visibility at this time.

Moore hesitated at first concerning Eliot's offer because of her "promise to Macmillan."[35] Eliot, however, was quick to explain that "the engagement with Macmillan does not interfere; they would take the American rights and we the British, that is all."[36]

Moore and Eliot then began a series of exchanges about the selection of the poems and the possibility of Eliot providing a preface to the volume. Eliot sent Frank Morley of Faber and Faber to call on Moore while he was in New York; during their visit, Moore suggested that Eliot write the preface.[37] Moore's suggestion was not surprising, given her enthusiastic response to Eliot's 1923 *Dial* essay about her work and her increasing respect for his criticism. But the tone of the letters they exchanged about this preface was unusual. They became, in a way that they had not been earlier, more reserved and somewhat stiff and overly deferential toward one another. It was as if they were consciously carving out the roles of parent and child that they would later adopt. In fact, their "private" exchanges sounded quite "public."

Eliot wrote to Moore on April 12, 1934, indicating that he now knew from Morley that she wished him to write the preface. He then added, almost in distrust of Moore's wishes: "Of course, I should be proud to contribute such a preface or introduction, if it was wanted but I should not think of doing so unless it was your express wish. Please do not allow politeness to prevent you from saying exactly what your preference is."[38] Moore had of course, as Eliot had himself acknowledged in the beginning of his letter, conveyed to him what her preference was. Nevertheless, her response on April 18, 1934, was characterized by politeness as she gave Eliot the option of bowing out of their nebulously formed agreement.

> Mr. Latham [of Macmillan] says something about an introduction by you as if it were a certainty. I had suggested it to Mr. Morley; to be based perhaps on your Dial article, but I have written Mr. Latham that I am not sure you would like to sponsor the book in that way or contribute more thinking than already has been involved.[39]

Eliot's sponsoring of her *Selected Poems* eventually becomes linked in both their minds with the book's success—with the financial profits the book might bring.[40] Eliot wrote to Moore on June 20, 1934, about the "prefatory eulogium" he was preparing to write.[41] Moore wrote back on July 2, pointing up the distance between herself and Eliot:

> Eulogism even used humorously makes me shrink to nothing. When my first things came out, I preserved lines of press comment that I happened on or that friends sent me. I liked them and did not think much about their having cost someone time and hard thinking. But I pale now at the thought of a champion's having to be like Joshua "a writer *and* [Moore's emphasis] a fighter."[42]

For Moore the launching of a text becomes inseparable from the critical commentary that accompanies it, or surrounds it. The critic is "a fighter" who promotes or advertises the author's work, and mediates between the author of the text and those who receive it. Moore's postscript to this July 2 letter is germane:

> P.P.S. Don't think from what I say about Joshua and his writing and his fighting that I suppose there is no royalty, if royalty is the term, for one who introduces and edits a book; but merely that I know the compensation is never adequate.[43]

While not exactly an author of Moore's book, Eliot is, Moore implies, a surrogate author or at least a parent of sorts whose critical apparatus becomes part of the text. Before the book was even published, Moore wrote to him in October of 1934: "I am venturing to hope there will be returns that can be shared with you."[44] And as we have seen, in September of 1935 Moore actually did try to share her returns—i.e., fifteen dollars—with Eliot.[45]

Moore not only viewed Eliot's introduction as part of the book, she also recognized the extent to which his prefatory remarks would be a seal of approval for the public. When she received the introduction in October of 1934 she wrote to Eliot about the effect it might have on the public:

> One could scarcely be human and not wish your Introduction might have the effect of a tidal wave, on the public, that it has had on me. The energy of thought that you bring to bear in behalf of this venture is the kind one summons in a case of fire or flood, and is a generosity the most self-ministering could not hope or pray for.[46]

Moore focuses on the effect Eliot's introduction may have on the public rather than on that which her book may have. Also, by comparing Eliot's energy to "the kind one summons in a case of fire or flood," she implicitly likens her own venture (the appearance of a book) to a natural disaster. Moore's text does not have an autonomous existence divorced from Eliot's preface.

Eliot was equally self-deprecating about his side of this venture. On June 28, 1934, he wrote to Moore about the inadequacy of all introductions:

> I am not very happy about my introduction but I don't believe that I should be satisfied even if it were much better. One feels something of the fatuity and superfluity of the chairman in after dinner speech-making: I am so conscious of an introduction being an impertinence, only justified by temporary considerations, that I am not happy in writing one.[47]

In October of the same year he referred to the introduction as "puny" and noted, "I dare say that it will seem to you a travesty."[48] When Moore reacted with great pleasure to the introduction, Eliot wrote back with diffidence: "I trust that your first impression, if it is what it appears to be, will survive. If you have any objections, you clothe them in a luminous and pleasing mist which makes them invisible."[49] Eliot unwittingly provided a description of much of Moore's criticism of her contemporaries. Nevertheless, his feigned insecurity in this response was a posture, for it can be documented that Eliot actually valued this essay very much.

Long after *Selected Poems* was published, the introduction continued to be an issue for both Moore and Eliot. It acquired the autonomy Moore never felt her *Selected Poems* had. In November of 1948 Eliot indicated that he hoped to have Moore's *Collected Poems* on the Faber and Faber list for 1949. Various delays ensued and in July 1950 we find Eliot writing to Moore: "I am perplexed what use to make of my old Preface to *Selected Poems*." He went on in a proprietary vein: "It still seems to me pretty satisfactory for the occasion, but I consider an introduction by another author an impertinence for a volume of Collected Poems. I might persuade myself, however, to quote it on the blurb with acknowledgements to myself." [50]

On August 4, 1950, Moore wrote back, telling him that he should certainly use his preface in whatever way he thought best; but even more important, she commented again on the significance of this preface for her own text.

> With regard to your Preface, I should on no account be allowed to be a woodman-turncoat against the wood that gave me a haft. I regard dust-covers as part of the library and indeed favor the expedient you suggest—to quote your Preface on the dust-cover with acknowledgement to yourself. Please do. . . .
> I have been inquired of by several persons concerning a collection by me of verse old and new. And the firm I favor has alluded several times to your Preface as an auspicious feature of such a collection. I said I would inquire if you can let the Preface be reprinted. As for its being an impertinence, it prompted me to attempt the collection. (Insisting implies that the material is not self-sustaining without the Preface. But this is true). [51]

Moore's dependence on Eliot cannot be underestimated; she still seems to feel that her material could not have stood on its own without Eliot's preface. The firm that she favored was Viking

Press, though Macmillan was still officially her American publisher. Viking Press was indeed savvy enough to know that Eliot's preface would be an important addition to Moore's collection. What is most significant about this letter is that fifteen years after *Selected Poems* was published Moore still felt the need for Eliot's public approval. She clearly felt more confident about offering her *Collected Poems* to the public with Eliot's blurb on the cover.

If Moore felt that Eliot's criticism of her work would protect her from a potentially unsupportive public, she certainly did not feel equipped to provide him with the same "armor." In fact, at times she seemed reticent to undertake the task of reviewing his work. "I should enjoy writing on your own recent poems," Moore wrote to Eliot at *The Criterion* in 1931, "but they doubtless have been commented on." [52]

Moore felt differently about the project of reviewing Stevens, Pound, and Williams. She seemed to believe, for example, that her reviews of Stevens might defend him from the "crass reader" [53] and "the wild boars of philistinism who rush about interfering with experts." [54] Her reviews of Pound might protect him from those critics and readers who misunderstood his poetic in the *Cantos*. Finally, although Moore was not always sanguine about her own ability to support Williams' enterprise, given their aesthetic differences, she took up his cause publicly when she reviewed his work, though privately she often expressed her reservations to him.

Eliot, on the other hand, after a certain point in his career did not seem to need Moore's or anyone else's defense. His enormous success can be dated to the 1922 publication of *The Waste Land*, which Moore never reviewed. Having reviewed Eliot's work twice before—once in 1918 and once in 1921—Moore probably could have taken on this project had she desired.

Her reviews of Eliot's work span her entire career: she reviewed his work six times between 1918 and 1952, encompassing the

range of his career as poet, critic, and dramatist.⁵⁵ Her 1921 re-
view of his *Sacred Wood* is unusual in that Moore is openly com-
bative, challenging at times some of Eliot's judgments. In her
1918 review of Eliot's *Prufrock and Other Observations*, Moore had
also hinted at potential differences between their respective aes-
thetics, though in subsequent reviews of Eliot's poetry—in 1931
and 1936—these differences are silenced or no longer in ques-
tion. Moore's search for a critical voice between 1918 and 1921
accounts in part for the tone of these two early reviews. It is also
possible that before Eliot came of age both as a critic and as a
poet Moore did not feel the need to assume a subordinate role to
him—to deny publicly her disagreements with him. By 1931,
however, when she reviewed his "Marina" (no. 29 of *The Ariel
Poems*), Moore had come to feel that her "appreciation" of his
work was somewhat superfluous, given Eliot's established posi-
tion. Also, her encroaching sense of dependence on Eliot un-
doubtedly made her reluctant to disagree openly with his choice
of subject matter or the tone with which he dealt with it. Eliot
had secured the public's approbation by this time in a way that
Stevens, Pound, Williams, and Moore had not.

In 1918, however, when Moore reviewed his first collection of
poems, *Prufrock and Other Observations*, for *Poetry*, Eliot's repu-
tation was virtually non-existent. I suspect that some of these
poems offended Moore, and given the tone of the review, it seems
odd that she even chose to review this collection. In fact, her
"Note on T. S. Eliot's Book" is not really a review at all, but
rather a reaction to the critical discourse that had recently been
generated by the appearance of Eliot's book. Notice the male per-
sona she adopts of "a hardened reviewer" to enter this critical
sphere and her need to position herself in the then-current debate
over "sentimentality" versus "realism" or honesty.

It might be advisable for Mr. Eliot to publish a fangless edi-
tion of *Prufrock and Other Observations* for the gentle reader who

likes his literature, like breakfast coffee or grapefruit, sweetened. A mere change in the arrangement of the poems would help a little. It might begin with *La Figlia che Piange*, followed perhaps by the *Portrait of a Lady*; for the gentle reader, in his eagerness for the customary bit of sweets, can be trusted to overlook the ungallantry, the youthful cruelty, of the substance of the "Portrait." It may as well be admitted that this hardened reviewer cursed the poet in his mind for this cruelty while reading the poem; and just when he was ready to find extenuating circumstances—the usual excuses about realism—out came this "drunken helot" (one can hardly blame the good English reviewer whom Ezra Pound quotes!) with that ending. It is hard to get over this ending with a few moments of thought; it wrenches a piece of life at the roots.[56]

Moore's highly stylized division between "the gentle reader" and "this hardened reviewer" allows her to appear to undermine the gentle reader and to join the ranks of certain truly hardened reviewers. But though she pokes fun at the reader who wishes *his* literature artificially sweetened and sets herself up as an experienced reviewer, it is clear that Moore, unlike the naive reader, cannot ignore the cruelty she confronts in Eliot's "Portrait of a Lady." She, unlike the reader she imagines, will not overlook moments like the ending of Eliot's "Portrait."

Despite her interest in this brand of realism, Moore identifies in part with the English reviewer whom Ezra Pound had quoted in his review of Eliot. She may not have actually read Arthur Waugh's review, "The New Poetry," which was published in *Quarterly Review* in October of 1916, but she most certainly read, or in any case heard about, Pound's response to this review which appeared in the *Egoist* in June of 1917. In "Drunken Helots and Mr. Eliot," Pound had identified Waugh as the subject of his attack and moved swiftly to his defense of Eliot:

Let us sample the works of the last "Drunken Helot." . . . Our
helot has a marvelous neatness. There is a comparable finesse
in Laforgue's "Votre ame est affaire d'oculiste," but hardly in
English verse. . . . And since when have helots taken to reading
Dante and Marlowe? Since when have helots made a new
music, a new refinement, a new method of turning old phrases
into new by their aptness?[57]

Although Pound's defense was eloquent enough, Moore pub-
licly allies herself with those seasoned reviewers who were un-
derstanding up to a point concerning the demands of realism,
until confronted with the ending of "Portrait." Moore, how-
ever, though not wholly comfortable with what Eliot is after in
these poems, praises Eliot's honesty in a way that Waugh would
not have.

Whistler in his post-impressionistic English studies—and these
poems are not entirely unlike Whistler's studies—had the ad-
vantage of his more static medium, of a somewhat more ro-
mantic temperament, and of the fact that the objects he painted
half-hid their ugliness under shadows and the haze of distance.
But Eliot deals with life, with beings and things who live and
move almost nakedly before his individual mind's eye. . . .
Whatever one may feel about sweetness in literature, there is
also the word honesty, and this man is a faithful friend of the
objects he portrays. . . .[58]

When Moore notes that Eliot's poems are like Whistler's studies
she may be echoing Pound's impulse to compare Eliot's work
to that of a painter. Pound maintained in a review of Eliot's poems
in 1917 that "the cold gray-green tones" of Velasquez have "an
emotional value not unlike the emotional value of Mr. Eliot's
rhythms, and of his vocabulary."[59] "If it is permitted to make
comparison with a different art," Pound asserted, "let me say that

he [Eliot] has used contemporary detail very much as Velasquez used contemporary detail. . . ." [60] More important, perhaps, Moore implies in her analogy that Eliot might well have taken a lesson from Whistler, who knew how to conceal the ugliness of his objects. Whistler, unlike Eliot, is able to disguise partially or half-hide the unpleasant associations of the objects he chose to paint; he accomplishes this by using shadows and perspective. Eliot, in contrast, having less of a romantic temperament, Moore implies, allows his subjects to move "almost nakedly" before him. Whistler's aesthetic of concealment thus stands in contrast to Eliot's of raw display. Moore's comparison allows her to hint that despite Eliot's honesty, she finds his vision a bit too revealing.

Three years later, in 1921, Moore reviewed Eliot's *Sacred Wood* for *The Dial*. She is self-assured in this review and is more comfortable responding to Eliot's criticism than to his poetry. As she celebrates Eliot's collection of essays, and occasionally takes issue with him, she defines and defends her own critical values.

When Eliot responded positively to Moore's review, she wrote back: "Your letter gives me great pleasure. In The Sacred Wood, I met so many enthusiasms of my own that I could not feel properly abashed to be 'criticizing' a critic—at least not until it was too late to retreat." [61] The tone of Moore's response, as well as the review itself, puts them on a curiously equal footing—one that by the thirties was no longer possible. Moore begins her 1921 review by identifying Eliot's definition of criticism:

As a revival of enjoyment it has value, but in what it reveals as a definition of criticism it is especially rich. The connection between criticism and creation is close; criticism naturally deals with creation but it is equally true that criticism inspires creation. A genuine achievement in criticism is an achievement in creation; as Mr. Eliot says, "It is to be expected that the critic and the creative artist should frequently be the same person." [62]

Moore's perhaps unconscious misreading of Eliot's position in "The Perfect Critic" makes Eliot's view of the critic, and criticism's function, closer to her own. When Eliot says at the end of "The Perfect Critic" that it is to be expected that the critic and the artist can be the same person, he maintains that "the two directions of sensibility are complementary," but not the same.[63] He does not assume as Moore does that an achievement in criticism could be, or could rival, a creative achievement. Moore's false accord here functions as a justification for her own creative translations of the writers she examines; it also allows her to give the critic and his discourse the kind of autonomy that Eliot and his followers bestow on the text or object of art.

What is interesting is that Moore's misreading makes Eliot sound in league with critics like Swinburne, Pater, and Symons, who really did seem to believe in creative criticism. This misreading is even more problematic since one of the things Eliot so eloquently does in *The Sacred Wood* is to sever any potential ties between his critical position and that of "impressionistic critics." In "Imperfect Critics," for example, Eliot describes Swinburne (one of the "impressionistic critics" he wished to dismiss) as a critic and maintains that he "was writing not to establish a critical reputation, not to instruct a docile public, but as a poet his notes upon poets whom he admired."[64] Eliot also concludes that "Swinburne is an appreciator and not a critic"[65] because he does not offer "judgments which can be reversed or even questioned. . . ."[66] In her review, Moore defends Swinburne both as a critic and as a poet:

What Mr. Eliot says of Swinburne as a critic, one feels to be true. "The content," of Swinburne's critical essays "is not, in any exact sense, criticism." Nor, we agree, is it offered by Swinburne as such; he wrote "as a poet, his notes upon poets whom he admired."[67]

At this stage in her own career as a critic/reviewer, Moore identi-
fied with Swinburne's desire to "write his notes." Later, certainly
by the thirties, in her reviews of poets such as Stevens and Pound,
Moore began to see her critical pieces on one level as attempts
"to instruct a docile public."

Moore's admiration of Swinburne can also be seen in her use
of a quotation from him that she employs to illuminate Eliot's
critical project:

> In his opening a door upon the past and indicating what is
> there, he recalls the comment made by Swinburne upon Hugo:
>   "Art knows nothing of death; . . . all that ever had life in it,
> has life in it for ever; those themes only are dead which never
> were other than dead. No form is obsolete, no subject out of
> date, if the right man be there to rehandle it." [68]

Moore's gesture of quoting Swinburne as a critic in order to
praise Eliot's rehandling of the past could not have been lost on
Eliot. This particular use of quotation—quoting one person on
someone else to reveal something about still a third person—
became a distinctive characteristic of Moore's critical method of
approaching her contemporaries. As she quotes Swinburne on
Hugo, Moore momentarily drops out of sight, fusing her own
judgment implicitly with Swinburne's and avoiding an overt disa-
greement with Eliot concerning the value of Swinburne's criti-
cism. For Moore there is a grace in avoiding a direct confronta-
tion with Eliot.

If Moore implicitly defended Swinburne as a critic, she overtly
disagreed with Eliot's reading of Swinburne as a poet. She does
not gloss over their aesthetic differences in this instance.

> Mr. Eliot allows Swinburne, perhaps, a sufficiently high place
> as a poet; to imply that he does not, is to disregard the posi-
> tively expressed acceptance of his genius; nevertheless, in the
> course of the essay on Swinburne as Poet, he says, "agreed that

we do not (and I think that the present generation does not) greatly enjoy Swinburne," et cetera. Do we not?[69]

Moore's rhetorical question frames in an assertive but innocuous way a rather elegant defense of Swinburne—a defense that focuses specifically on Eliot's objections. "There is about Swinburne," she maintains, "the atmosphere of magnificence, a kind of permanent association of him with King Solomon 'perfumed with all the powders of the merchants, approaching in his litter'— an atmosphere which is not destroyed, one feels, even by indiscriminate browsing. . . ."[70] Moore's extravagant metaphor for Swinburne's magnificence serves to deflate Eliot's more serious objections to Swinburne's poetry. She is probably also responding to Eliot's contention that "almost no one, today, will wish to read the whole of Swinburne. It is not because Swinburne is voluminous; certain poets, equally voluminous, must be read entire."[71]

Moore also takes issue with Eliot's belief that "when you take to pieces any verse of Swinburne, you find always that the object was not there—only the word."[72] She counters Eliot's judgment with her own carefully chosen examples from Swinburne:

As for "the word" however, invariably used by him as a substitute for "the object," is it always so used? . . . What of

"The sea slow rising
. . . .
the rocks that shrink,
the fair brave trees with all their flowers at play?"[73]

Moore's rhetorical question is again a polite but firm way of framing her refutation of Eliot; the examples she offers, rather than extended explanations, also function in this way. She offers her quotations from Swinburne without providing a reading of them.

After discussing Swinburne at some length, she concludes:

"One of the chief charms, however, of Mr. Eliot's criticism is that in his withholding of praise, an author would feel no pain."[74] Moore retreats here from becoming publicly embattled; furthermore, she and Eliot never engaged in a private exchange concerning their disagreement over Swinburne's enterprise.

Moore ends her review with what appears to be a reference to the balance between Eliot's criticism and poetry: "In his poetry, he seems to move troutlike through a multiplicity of foreign objects and in his instinctiveness and care as a critic, he appears as a complement to the sheen upon his poetry."[75] Moore's critique of Eliot's temperament is perceptive and compelling. In her image of Eliot moving like a trout through a world of foreign objects, she captures Eliot's detachment and remoteness from the world he tries to inhabit and create; Moore implies that Eliot is only half at home, despite his graceful movements, in this world of foreign objects. She also hints that it may be hard for readers to see Eliot in his world, for a trout's movements are hard to follow. (In his biography of Eliot, Peter Ackroyd also points to Eliot's cultivated aloofness and elusiveness: "He cultivated such distance and detachment as if by not fully belonging, or wholly participating, something of himself was preserved—something secret and inviolable which he could nourish. The idea of isolation and invulnerability was clearly very important to him, and in letters to friends such as Conrad Aiken and Mary Hutchinson he sometimes conjures up images of submarine depths—of their coolness and remoteness."[76])

An earlier unpublished version of Moore's image of Eliot moving "troutlike" through his world sheds some light on the necessary distance Moore feels Eliot maintains. In "English Literature Since 1914," an unpublished essay of 1920, we find the first version of this passage:

> The sheen upon T. S. Eliot's poems, the facile troutlike passage of his mind through a multiplicity of foreign objects recall

the "spic torrent" in Wallace Stevens' Pecksniffiana. Mr. Eliot
does not mar his subject by overdoing it and he does not bring
too heavy a touch to bear on it. His nonchalance together with
his power of implication make him one of the definite spirits of
the time.[77]

Moore praises Eliot's reserve and his aloofness in a way in which
she will later praise Stevens' same habit of mind. This is Moore's
earliest comparison, tentatively made, between Eliot and Ste-
vens.[78] Her other comparisons are also worth briefly examining.

In Moore's reading notebook for 1921−22 she indicates that
she had been reading Stevens' poetry in *Poetry* (October 1921);
beside Stevens' title, "On the Manner of Addressing Clouds," we
find the notation "cf. T. S. Eliot."[79] Also, in the four pages of
loose notes in the back of Moore's copy of Stevens' *Harmonium*
(notes that Moore used when composing her reviews of Stevens),
we find several references to Eliot. For example, beside two lines
from Stevens' "Le Monocle de Mon Oncle"—"Or was it that I
mocked myself alone? / I wish that I might be a thinking stone"—
we find the notation "cf Prufrock." There is also a reference to
Crispin's journey through "the harbor streets." Beside this, Moore
has written "T. S. Eliot."[80] In 1937 in her review of Stevens' *Owl's
Clover* Moore compares Eliot and Stevens:

> We feel, in the tentatively detached method of implication, the
> influence of Plato; and an awareness of if not the influence of
> T. S. Eliot. Better say that each has influenced the other; with
> *Sunday Morning* and the Prufrocklike lines in *Le Monocle de Mon
> Oncle* in mind, . . . and the Peter Quince−like rhythmic contour
> of T. S. Eliot's *La Figlia che Piange*. As if it were Antipholus of
> Ephesus and Antipholus of Syracuse, each has an almost too
> acute concept of "the revenge of music"; a realization that
> the seducer is the seduced; and a smiling, strict, Voltaire-like,
> straight-seeing, self-directed humor which triumphs in its pain.

Each is engaged in a similar though differently expressed search for that which will endure.[81]

Although Moore suggests here that Eliot and Stevens are twins of sorts, in her 1918 review of *Prufrock and Other Observations* she certainly had reservations about Eliot's "self-directed humor" and cruelty in poems like "Portrait." She had, as we recall, suggested "a fangless edition" of *Prufrock and Other Observations*. Stevens, in contrast, can satirize himself in an often melancholy, self-indulgent fashion and escape the implications of such a gesture by employing "his method of hints and disguises."

In 1931 Moore reviewed Eliot's poetry for the second time, focusing this time in her review of "Marina" on Eliot's temperament as well as his method of coping with his desperations. Moore begins by noting: "The theme is frustration and frustration is pain."[82] Yet despite this frustration, this is a poem, she reminds us, about renunciation: "Not sumptuous grossness but a burnished hedonism is renounced."[83] Moore recognizes that Eliot's renunciation is earned. She then points to the distance he necessarily maintains between himself and his readers, particularly those readers who become fixated on sharing his frustrations.

Those who naively proffer consolation put the author beyond their reach, in initiate solitude. Although solitude is to T. S. Eliot, we infer, not "a monarchy of death," each has his private desperations; a poem may mean one thing to the author and another to the reader. What matters here is that we have, for both author and reader, a machinery of satisfaction that is powerfully affecting, intrinsically and by association.[84]

Moore suggests here that Eliot's project demands that he keep his distance. Nevertheless, we as readers, and here I believe Moore includes herself, have our own desperations and these Moore maintains will not intersect with Eliot's. Eliot eludes us—is finally, with his troutlike movements, beyond our reach. Eliot's "machinery" (a curiously mechanical image for the deeply personal nature of this poem), we may infer, protects him, as Moore's "minor subjects" do, from those who wish to console him.

Moore then gives us a catalogue of the characteristics of Eliot's method. Distancing herself from Eliot's pain, Moore describes with precision Eliot's technique:

> The method is a main part of the pleasure: lean cartography; reiteration with compactness; emphasis by word pattern rather than by punctuation; the conjoining of opposites to produce irony; a counterfeiting verbally of the systole, diastole, of sensation—of what the eye sees and the mind feels; . . . As part of the revising of conventionality in presentment there is the embedded rhyme, evincing dissatisfaction with bald rhyme. This hiding, qualifying, and emphasizing of rhyme to an adjusted tempo is acutely a pleasure besides being a clue to feeling that is the source, as in *Ash Wednesday*, of harmonic contour like the sailing descent of the eagle.[85]

Retreating from her highly perceptive formalist analysis, Moore attempts to reconcile Eliot's readers to his "vogue for torment"; her final paragraph is not unlike the final one in her 1918 review in which she had praised Eliot's honesty.

> *Marina* is not for those who read inquisitively, as a compliment to the author, or to find material for the lecture platform. . . . If charged by chameleon logic and unstudious didactism with creating a vogue for torment, Mr. Eliot can afford not to be incommoded, knowing that his work is the testament of one "having to construct something upon which to rejoice."[86]

Eliot, Moore suggests, does not need anyone's defense. This passage is also reminiscent of her contention that Stevens refused to cater to his readers' expectations.

On June 16, 1934, Moore wrote to Eliot: "It is good of you to send me *The Rock*. The effect of repose and meditation despite the various kinds of effort that must have gone to [*sic*] it, is really a marvel."[87] Two years later, Moore reviewed Eliot's poetry again. In her 1936 review of his *Collected Poems,* she also stresses the aesthetic balance Eliot strives for: between the effect of repose and the concealment of the effort that went into accomplishing this. Eliot's aesthetic, in this instance, is in keeping with Moore's.

> Those who have power to renounce life are those whose lives are valuable to a community; one who attains equilibrium in spite of opposition to himself from within is in a stronger position than if there had been no opposition to overcome; and in art, freedom evolving from a liberated constraint is stronger than if it had not by nature been cramped. Indigenous skepticism, also constraint are part of Mr. Eliot's temperament; but at its apex art is able to conceal the artist while it exhibits his "angel"; like the unanticipatedly limber florescence of fireworks as they expand into trees or bouquets with the abandon of "unbroke horses". . . .[88]

Moore's second sentence in this passage mirrors in its structure the energy she identifies in Eliot's poetic. She earns her freedom in this sentence as she maintains Eliot does in his work. Her sentence has the appearance of constraint or limits in it until she shifts from what appears to be a simile to a metaphor for the artist's divine self or genius. In the first part of the sentence we are in a mind, processing information as it goes along: "Indigenous skepticism, / also constraint / are part of Mr. Eliot's temperament; / but at its apex / art is able to conceal the artist / while it exhibits his 'angel'. . . ." In Moore's sentence, like a seventeenth-century baroque period, we have the appearance of an unexpected internal explosion within the sentence itself as the metaphor unfolds. The artist's divine self is likened to the unanticipated appearance of fireworks which expand in such a way that they become reminiscent of the freedom exhibited by "'unbroke horses.'" Moore's own "liberated constraint" competes with Eliot's as she fuses sight and sound, linking the sudden and short-lived appearance of the fireworks to the equally unpredictable "abandon of 'unbroke horses.'"

Moore also returns in this review to the balance in Eliot's enterprise between his poetry and his criticism: "Although as a critic, confronted by apparent misapprehension, he manifests what seems at times an almost pugnacious sincerity, by doing his fighting in prose he is perhaps the more free to do his feeling in verse."[89] The phrase "pugnacious sincerity," which later becomes "combative sincerity" in the version of this review Moore published in *Predilections*, captures the split and balance in Eliot between "his fighting in prose" and "his feeling in verse." In a 1926 *Dial* "Comment" Moore had stressed the "studious constraint" and "inherent equilibrium" Eliot achieves as a critic: "By no means wearily yet warily, we examine generalizations with regard to poetry, and unimpaired by their studious constraint, T. S. Eliot's epitomes and hypotheses are in their inherent equilibrium, detaining."[90] There is a cautiousness and constraint in the balances of the sentence that is undermined by the effect of the adjectival modifier "detaining." Moore startles us here in the same way that Eliot's epitomes and hypotheses may, despite the surface appearance of equilibrium.

In her 1936 review, Moore is also concerned with the balance Eliot achieves between certain opposites: "For him hell is hell in its awareness of heaven; good is good in its distinctness from evil; precision is precision as triumphing over vagueness."[91] Later in the review she adds: "He has not dishonored 'the deepest terrors and desires,' depths of 'degradation' and heights of 'exaltation,' or the fact that it is possible to have 'walked in hell' and 'been rapt to heaven.'"[92] Moore highlights the moral dimension of Eliot's vision, without dismissing the struggle which accompanies it.

Although Moore expressed an interest in Eliot's "mental chronology of evolvement and deepening technique" in her 1936 review of his *Collected Poems*, she never reviewed his poetry again.

During the thirties she reviewed two of Eliot's plays: *Sweeney Agonistes* in 1933 and *Murder in the Cathedral* in 1936. Moore chose, however, not to review Eliot's *Four Quartets*, all of which had been published by 1942. We can only speculate about why she decided not to review any of them. As I have suggested, Moore was more committed to exploring Eliot's critical enterprise than she was to considering his poetic one. It was Eliot's "Reticent Candor" in his criticism that she praised as late as 1952; we notice in this essay that Moore takes something Conrad Aiken said about *The Waste Land* and applies it to Eliot's prose: "Reviewing *The Waste Land*, Conrad Aiken said, 'T. S. Eliot's net is wide and the meshes are small. . . .'; especially wide and small as prose bearing on poetry."[93]

Moore covered the range of Eliot's talent between 1918 and 1952, reviewing his poetry, drama, and criticism, though finally it was his concern "from the first with the art and use of poetry"[94] in his criticism that drew her to him. Given Eliot's incisive readings of Moore's own poetry in 1923 and again in 1935, it is not surprising that she valued his criticism so much.

Afterword

If I may venture to say again what I have already said when
obscurity was deplored, one should be as clear as one's natural
reticence allows one to be.[1]

My study of Marianne Moore's public and private literary
exchanges with her contemporaries—Stevens, Pound, Williams,
and Eliot—seeks to resituate her in the high modernist commu-
nity and to show that her criticism of these four poets constitutes
a major contribution to the canon of modern American critical
discourse about poetry. Moore operates in the world of Eliot and
Blackmur, yet she is subversive of most of the New Critical as-
sumptions we have inherited from them. If Eliot and Blackmur
champion the possibility of "close reading," valorizing the object
of art as autonomous, Moore, with her emphasis on the "reader"
and writer of the text rather than the text, elevates her own trans-
lation or new text over the work she examines. She makes us
reconsider what a text is. Instead of thinking of a work of art as
stable and of criticism as a discourse that prompts us, as Black-
mur maintains it should, to "return to the verse itself in its own
language,"[2] Moore assumes that every reading is potentially
capable of creating the text. Reading in her scheme becomes cre-
ative in its own right, as she dissolves the assumed division be-
tween her text and the one she examines.

Breaking down Eliot's distinction between "criticism and cre-
ation," Moore's reviews create not only new texts, but ones that
often compete with the originals. In her reviews of Stevens, Pound,
Williams, and Eliot, Moore collapses Eliot's distinction in two

ways. Commentary often takes the form of imitative appreciation, in which Moore copies in her own writing some quality of the writer's temperament or aesthetic she admires or feels ambivalent about. This device, as I have pointed out, allows her both to endorse the writer under consideration and to keep her distance. Moore also offers a mosaic of quotations from the text she is reviewing, from the writer's other work, and from others who have commented on the writer under review. This arrangement then becomes a "new" and potentially competing text. Both of these aspects of her style position Moore at a calculated distance from her subjects. As I have demonstrated, Moore appeared increasingly to cultivate this aloofness, recognizing that her aesthetic disclosures were most possible in the moments that she was most concealed.

Her criticism also fulfills in part Gerald Bruns' definition of "rhetorical improvisation":

> Rhetorical improvisation is related to embellishment and ornamentation; it is an art of doing something to what has already been done. In music and poetry it is a way of exceeding what is written by working between the lines or in the margin, or by using the text as a point of departure or as a program of intervals. Improvisation in this case is not an art of free origination; it begins instead with what is received, which it then proceeds to color, amplify, or fulfill, never to abolish or forget.[3]

Moore's reviews are improvisation in the sense that they have the appearance of having been "written to the moment." It is as if she is discovering her course—making up her text—as she goes along. As with a seventeenth-century "meditation" we are in a mind that revels in the performance of discovery. Her lack of expository conventions also reminds us of what Bruns calls "the unpredictability of improvisational discourse."[4] "The improvisation is ungeneric," he maintains, "precisely to the extent that it confounds those signals that we normally use to complete the text we have not finished reading; it dismantles the virtual or heuristic whole that we need to construct in order to guide ourselves. . . ."[5] Although Bruns asserts that "improvisations tend to occur at the level of the discourse, not at the level of the sentence,"[6] Moore's improvisations or meditations, like those of Montaigne, Bacon, Burton, or Emerson, work at the level of the sentence and sometimes even at the level of the phrase. This highlighting of the fragment accounts for the nonlinear movement and the multiplicity of perspectives in her critical discourse. Moore's multiple perspectives continually call into question our glimpse of the whole. She asks us to take the part as representative of the whole; as with Joyce's vision of the gnomon, Moore suggests that we "know" things by their shadows.

Williams, Eliot, and Stevens all comment on Moore's tendency to focus on the fragment in her poetry. In 1925 when Williams notes that one encounters in her work a view of "a flaw, a crack in the bowl,"[7] he defines an aesthetic that can no longer subscribe to "romantic" notions of wholeness, unity, or completeness. The flaw or crack in the object—that which destroys or divides—becomes inseparable from "knowing" the object itself; "destruction and creation," as Williams asserts, "are simultaneous."[8] In 1935 Eliot identifies Moore's use of "minute detail rather than that of emotional unity."[9] It seemed to be Eliot's consistent interest in emotional unity that made Moore uncomfortable when she approached his poetry. If Williams demands that we direct our attention to the fissure in the bowl rather than the bowl itself, Eliot suggests that we look closely at the "details" Moore uses in approaching her subjects. Moore's various approaches to the object, Eliot contends, "make us see the object more clearly, though we may not understand immediately why our attention has been called to this object, and though we may not immediately grasp its association with a number of other objects."[10] Her method also makes her objects "a little hard to see."[11] Stevens also acknowledges this in his 1935 review of her

Selected Poems when he implies that in "The Steeple-Jack" Moore gives us "the tropics at first hand" by showing us both what can be seen and what cannot. Moore complements Stevens' vision in "Notes Toward a Supreme Fiction": "It must be visible or invisible, / Invisible or visible or both: / A seeing and unseeing in the eye."

For Stevens, Moore's "romantic" is connected to her ability to privilege the fragment without losing sight of the fact that "an object [is] the sum of its complications, seen / And unseen."[12] Stevens and Moore are both committed to an exploration of the "complications" that necessarily surround any object or perception. As Stevens notes in his 1935 review of Moore's *Selected Poems*, "Moon-vines are moon-vines and tedious. But moon-vines trained on fishing-twine are something else. . . ."[13] Not surprisingly, Williams is judged harshly by both Stevens and Moore for abandoning his early belief that objects/fragments come alive in their surroundings because of their intricate relationships.

The aesthetic I have been defining accounts for Moore's strong endorsement of Stevens and Pound. It also explains why she became increasingly disillusioned with Williams' work, particularly after *Kora in Hell*. We can also see why she had reservations with Eliot's early poetic enterprise. Moore's quiet and often disguised "writing off" of Williams and Eliot, then, can best be understood in the context of her celebration of Stevens' and Pound's aesthetics.

Although Pound and Eliot are usually grouped together, primarily because of their commitment to an historical project, Moore implicitly links Stevens and Pound together. For her, Stevens and Pound, more than any other moderns, shared her own preference for the fragment, the shifting voice, the unspoken or invisible, that which cannot be predicted, the changing, always shifting perspective, and the unmasking and masking of the self. Mirroring in her own style Stevens' "bravura" and Pound's "love of risk," Moore seems to have found an analogue for Stevens' evasiveness in Pound's need to take risks. We see this when she returns in her reviews of Pound's *Cantos* in the thirties to the same images and metaphors she had used to discuss Stevens' *Harmonium* in 1924.

It is noteworthy that what Blackmur objected to in Pound was precisely what Moore valued in his work. Pound challenged Blackmur's notions of what a text might consist of: "It is not the kind of content that can be analyzed—because, separated, its components retain no being."[14] Blackmur found that Pound's fragments and "many voices"[15] "are not arrayed by logic or driven by pursuing emotion, they are connected because they follow one another. . . ."[16] In short, Pound's *Cantos* would not submit themselves to the type of analysis Blackmur practiced. Eliot's many allusions are acceptable to Blackmur because he, unlike Pound, "moulds wholes out of parts themselves autonomous."[17] Blackmur also extracts a wholeness of vision out of Stevens: "Mr. Stevens, not a dramatic poet, seizes his wholes only in imagination; in his poems the parts are already connected."[18] In contrast, he defines Pound's method in terms of its discontinuity: "This deliberate disconnectedness, this art of a thing continually alluding to itself, continually breaking off short, is the method by which the Cantos tie themselves together."[19] Moore of course found a method of celebrating Pound's discontinuous style by weaving fragments from Pound's prose as well as his poetry into her own commentary, and by miming in her own style his tendency to thwart our expectations.

She could celebrate in a way that Blackmur never could the "minute detail" or "the parts" of the whole that Stevens and Pound both employ. Stevens' imagery was opulent for Moore because it was "frugally unified." Stevens celebrates the roving eye rather than a fixed "I." We see this particularly in poems from *Harmonium* such as "Nomad Exquisite," "Six Significant Landscapes," and "Tea at the Palaz of Hoon." We experience an eye that renews its vision in the impermanence of the moment, or in the conviction that only that which passes can have any aesthetic permanence. Stevens' scarcely unified yet richly suggestive imagery, like Moore's metaphor for it—her night-blooming cereus—makes us see "a permanence composed of impermanence."

Williams failed for Moore (and for Stevens) because he lost the alertness of his early vision. When Moore first reviewed him in 1921, she compared his enterprise to that of Sir Francis Bacon, maintaining that Williams, like Bacon, had "the ability to see resemblances in things which are dissimilar."[20] She also praised Williams for "his power over the actual"—for his talent "to fix the atmosphere of a moment."[21] At this point Moore believed that Williams, despite his occasional displays of "aesthetic anarchy,"[22] was committed, as she and Stevens were, to transforming the quotidian. By 1934, Moore was convinced that Williams had abandoned this aesthetic. When she reviewed his *Collected Poems* in 1934, Moore hinted that Williams registered but failed to transform "things others never notice." She also maintained that "he is at times insultingly unevasive."[23] Williams' eye, Moore implied, had become lazy. By the time he finished *Paterson*, Williams still valued the possibilities afforded by focusing intently on the fragment—what he had called Pound's "shot through all material" or Moore's "anthology of transit"—but he had abandoned any but the most occasional pretense of "romanticizing" it. The important aesthetic differences I have established between Moore and Williams should end the critical insistence that Moore shared Williams' faith in "no ideas but in things."

There was a rawness in Eliot's early poetry with which I suspect Moore could not come to terms. In addition, Eliot's desire for emotional unity—a desire that critics like Blackmur and Matthiessen acknowledged and praised—seemed to make Moore uneasy. When she reviewed his later poetry Moore focused almost exclusively on his technique, as if she were in flight from Eliot's "private desperations."

Moore seemed particularly troubled by overt expressions of emotion. As she suggested in a 1944 letter to Williams, cited earlier, Stevens' examination of and by extension flirtation with what Vendler calls self-pity in his "Esthétique du Mal" made her uncomfortable.[24] Moore, however, does not usually feel the need to censor Stevens publicly for his occasional tendencies to be melancholy or to satirize himself in poems like "Le Monocle de Mon Oncle." Presumably, Stevens' different disguises allowed him to confront and avoid a poetic aesthetic of emotional confrontation. Eliot, in contrast, did not maintain this necessary distance. For Moore, Eliot's "romantic" journey toward the self and its frustrations was much too direct.

Moore's preference for Stevens and Pound over Williams and Eliot and her critical method of exploring these predilections exemplify an aesthetic that thrives on hints, masks, and partial revelations or disclosures. Moore's letters to her contemporaries and her reviews of their work highlight the tension between what she believes she can disclose and what she feels she must veil or merely hint at; this tension reflects the central core of Moore's epistemology, one in which "things" are known through partial glimpses or fragmented revelations. It also informs her distinctive aesthetic—one that enables her to reveal and to conserve her self. In recovering the link between this economy of self-expenditure and self-preservation, I have sought to illuminate a vital aspect of Moore's aesthetic and temperament, and to reconstruct an essential chapter in the history of modern American poetry.

Permissions

Notes

1. *"Breasting the mode":*
Moore's Place in High Modernism

1. Moore, "Idiosyncrasy and Technique," in *A Marianne Moore Reader*, 178.
2. Rosenbach Museum and Library, VI:21:13, A.L.S., Marianne Moore to John Warner Moore, December 16, 1915. Although Moore was hesitant at this time to take on the task of reviewing music, sport and dancing, many of the metaphors in her later reviews in fact come from these discourses.
3. Moore, "Samuel Butler."
4. Moore, "The Accented Syllable."
5. See Rosenbach Museum and Library, II:05:08, Moore, unpublished prose, "Poe, Byron, and Bacon," 1916.
6. See Rosenbach Museum and Library, V:17:16, A.L.S., Harriet Shaw Weaver to Marianne Moore, December 9, 1916.
7. Moore's poetry has certainly received critical attention. For a representative selection of her early reception by Pound, Eliot, and Williams, see *Marianne Moore: A Collection of Critical Essays*, ed. Charles Tomlinson. For a less positive early reception of Moore's work, see Harriet Monroe, "Symposium on Marianne Moore." For an overview of Moore's post-modernist reception, see the Marianne Moore Issue of *Quarterly Review of Literature*, 4 (No. 2) (1948), 153–69. Recent studies of Moore's poetic achievement include Bernard F. Engel, *Marianne Moore*; A. Kingsley Weatherhead, *The Edge of the Image: Marianne Moore, William Carlos Williams and Some Other Poets*; George Nitchie, *Marianne Moore: An Introduction to the Poetry*; Donald Hall, *Marianne Moore: The Cage and the Animal*; Laurence Stapleton, *Marianne Moore: The Poet's Advance*; Bonnie Costello, *Marianne*

Moore: Imaginary Possessions; John Slatin, *The Savage's Romance: The Poetry of Marianne Moore*; Grace Shulman, *Marianne Moore: The Poetry of Engagement*; Taffy Martin, *Marianne Moore: Subversive Modernist*; Margaret Holley, *The Poetry of Marianne Moore: A Study in Voice and Value*. See also *Twentieth Century Literature*, 30 (Marianne Moore Issue) (Summer/Fall 1984). See also *The Complete Prose of Marianne Moore*, ed. Patricia C. Willis. See also two recent reviews of Moore's prose: Denis Donoghue, "She's Got Rhythm," *New York Review of Books*, December 4, 1986, 40–44; Helen Vendler, "Poet's Prose," *New Yorker*, March 16, 1987, 94–96.

8. Kenneth Burke, "Likings of an Observationalist," rpt. in Tomlinson, *Marianne Moore: A Collection of Critical Essays*, 125.

9. Ibid.

10. Randall Jarrell, *Kipling, Auden & Co.: Essays and Reviews 1935–1964*, 215.

11. Stapleton, *Marianne Moore: The Poet's Advance*, 52.

12. Costello, *Marianne Moore: Imaginary Possessions*, 215.

13. Ibid., 216.

14. Hall, *Marianne Moore: The Cage and the Animal*, 135.

15. There are three important studies that consider Moore's role at *The Dial*: William Wasserstrom, *The Time of the Dial*; Nicholas Joost, *Scofield Thayer and The Dial: An Illustrated History*; and Taffy Martin, "Preparation and Enactment: Marianne Moore's Editorship of *The Dial*."

16. Rosenbach Museum and Library, V:54:30, A.L.S., Marianne Moore to George Saintsbury, August 30, 1926.

17. Another reason editorial decisions cannot be attributed to Moore alone is that many of the decisions seem to have been discussed in the office or were made in consultation through the mail with James Sibley Watson. Also it appears to have been a *Dial* policy to say little or nothing concerning why something was rejected; carbons of Moore's responses (housed in the *Dial* archive at the Beinecke Library at Yale University and in the Watson Papers at the Berg Collection at the New York Public Library) to potential and actual contributors rarely discuss the reasons for her decisions. Therefore, speculations concerning her own values based on her work at *The Dial* are problematic.

18. There are several important essays concerning Moore and Bishop: Lynn Keller, "Words Worth a Thousand Postcards: The Bishop/ Moore Correspondence"; David Kalstone, "Trial Balances: Elizabeth Bishop and Marianne Moore"; and Bonnie Costello, "Marianne Moore and Elizabeth Bishop: Friendship and Influence." For an excellent discussion of H.D. and Moore, see Margaret M. Phelan, "H.D. and M.M.: Correspondences and Contradictions."

19. I am thinking here of her reviews and not of her essays or "Comments" in *The Dial*. Stapleton also calls attention to the unique quality of Moore's decision to focus on her contemporaries; see *Marianne Moore: The Poet's Advance*, 54.

20. Vendler, "Poet's Prose," 95.

21. See Rosenbach Museum and Library, V:17:26, T.L.C., Marianne Moore to T. S. Eliot, June 27, 1935. Much of their correspondence during the thirties supports my argument. For a fuller treatment of this subject see chapter 5.

22. Louise Bogan was the only one of Moore's early critics to mention that Moore did not always praise her subjects. See Bogan, "*Predilections*," *New Yorker*, 30 July 1955, 67–68. Bogan asserted that Moore "has a sharp ear for the false note and can chide as well as commend." Most recently, Vendler maintained: "Because Moore preferred whenever possible to write appreciatively, her sardonic powers are kept in restraint here [in *The Complete Prose*], but the alert reader will find sly rebukes to presuming authors. . . ." ("Poet's Prose," 95).

23. Moore refers to Stevens' "achieved remoteness" in her first review of his work: "Well Moused, Lion," 84. She refers to "his method of hints and disguises" and his "bravura" in her review of *Owl's Clover* and *Ideas of Order*, "Unanimity and Fortitude." The phrases "firm piloting" and "rebellious fluency" can be found in Moore's second review of Pound's *Cantos*: "A Draft of XXX Cantos," 482.

24. I am quoting Moore who is quoting Pound on Henry James. See "The Cantos," 47.

25. Glenway Wescott, "A Succession of Poets," 399.

26. For an important discussion of this issue, see Alicia S. Ostriker, *Stealing the Language: The Emergence of Women's Poetry in America*.

27. Wescott, "A Succession of Poets," 400.

28. See also Martin, *Marianne Moore: Subversive Modernist*. Martin argues (p. 3) that Moore's cultivated public image of herself as docile, retiring, reticent and noncombative has hindered critics who "often treat her as a decorative oddity rather than as an active and perhaps even dangerous force."

29. Jarrell, "Her Shield," rpt. in Tomlinson, ed., *Marianne Moore: A Collection of Critical Essays*, 114–24.

30. Costello, *Marianne Moore: Imaginary Possessions*, 108.

31. Ibid., 108–9.

32. In "Towards a Poetics of Disclosure: Marianne Moore and Henry James," I argue that Moore's aesthetic was influenced by the one James endorsed in his memoir, *A Small Boy and Others* (1913). Moore pays tribute directly to the relationship between James' temperament and aesthetic in her 1934 essay about him and indirectly in her 1924 poem, "An Octopus."

33. Ostriker, *Stealing the Language*, 52.

34. Ibid., 53.

35. Ibid.

36. See Martin, *Marianne Moore: Subversive Modernist*. Martin argues that Moore herself cultivated the myth that she was a harmless spinster in a tricorne; she also points out that this myth still serves to prevent critics from recovering Moore's radical yet central place in this community.

37. Ibid., xiii: "Moore's unpublished correspondence, her reading notebooks, her workbooks, and several romans à clef portraying Moore help to correct the lopsided impression that she was little more than a teetotaling, feminine mascot for the bohemian Greenwich Village writers who confronted modernism singlehandedly."

38. Rosenbach Museum and Library, II:02:14, Draft Notes for "Feeling and Precision," 1934.

39. For discussions of Moore's ambition, see Martin, *Marianne Moore: Subversive Modernist*; Ostriker, *Stealing the Language: The Emergence of Women's Poetry in America*; Phelan, "H.D. and M.M.: Correspondences and Contradictions"; and Slatin, *The Savage's Romance: The Poetry of Marianne Moore*.

40. Phelan, "H.D. and M.M.: Correspondences and Contradictions," 4–8.

41. Ostriker, *Stealing the Language*, 52.
42. Rosenbach Museum and Library, V:54:32, T.L.C., Marianne Moore to George Saintsbury, September 14, 1928.
43. See Patricia C. Willis, "Marianne Moore and Peter Morris: Facts and Speculations."
44. Ibid., 14.
45. Rosenbach Museum and Library, V:38:26, T.L.C., Marianne Moore to H. S. Latham, September 28, 1933.
46. Rosenbach Museum and Library, V:02:47, T.L.C., Marianne Moore to W. H. Auden, October 12, 1944.
47. Moore, *Predilections*, vii.
48. Burke refers to Moore's criticism of Williams as a mixture of "an almost pedantic literalness with the moodiness of impressionistic criticism" in "Likings of an Observationalist," rpt. in *Marianne Moore: A Collection of Critical Essays*, 127. There is evidence that Moore thought highly of both Swinburne's and Symons' prose. See Rosenbach Museum and Library, VII:01:02, 1250/2, Reading Notebook 1916–1921, where in 1917 Moore refers to Swinburne on Arnold, Byron, Chaucer, Coleridge, and Hugo. In Rosenbach Museum and Library, VII:01:03, 1250/3, Reading Notebook 1921–1922, we find a reference in 1921 to Symons' *Key of Blue* and his essay on Beardsley. In addition, in some notes labelled Prose Metaphors and Similes (see Rosenbach Museum and Library, VII:09:05, Prose Metaphors and Similes 1918–1929), Moore has copied passages from Swinburne's and Symons' "criticism."
49. I am thinking here of Derrida, Barthes, and Hartman, all of whom attempt in different ways to break down the division between literary commentary and the original text that inspired it. Harold Bloom and others have explored Pater's relevance to "modernists," "postmodernists," and contemporary criticism. See Bloom, ed., *Selected Writings of Walter Pater*, vii–xxxi. See also William K. Wimsatt and Cleanth Brooks, *Literary Criticism: A Short History*, vol. 2, *Romantic and Modern Criticism*, 493–96. They provide a brief sketch of "impressionistic" criticism.
50. T. S. Eliot, *The Selected Prose of T. S. Eliot*, 73–74.
51. Geoffrey Hartman, *Criticism in the Wilderness: The Study of Literature Today*, 189.

52. Ibid.

53. Rosenbach Museum and Library, V:23:32, T.L.S., H.D. to Marianne Moore, August 1, 1925.

54. Hartman, *Criticism in the Wilderness*, 36.

55. Ibid., 201. See also Hartman, *Saving the Text: Literature/Derrida/ Philosophy*, xviii: Hartman maintains that Derrida's *Glas* "is recognizably a commentary on Hegel and Genet, yet it does not remain subordinate to them. . . ."

56. Moore, "Archaically New," 83.

57. Moore, "The Poem and the Print," *Poetry*, 95.

58. Eliot, *Selected Prose of T. S. Eliot*, 69.

59. Eliot, *The Sacred Wood: Essays on Poetry and Criticism*, 2–3.

60. Walter Pater, preface to *The Renaissance*, xx.

61. Quoted in Richard Ellman, introduction to *The Artist as Critic: Critical Writings of Oscar Wilde*, ed. Ellman (New York: Random House, 1968), xii.

62. Eliot, *The Sacred Wood*, 5–6.

63. See the discussion of Eliot's "The Perfect Critic" in Wimsatt and Brooks, 658–59.

64. Burke, "Likings of an Observationalist," rpt. in *Marianne Moore: A Collection of Critical Essays*, 127.

65. Ibid., 125.

66. Rosenbach Museum and Library, LNH, Moore's copy of Saintsbury, *The Collected Essays and Papers of George Saintsbury 1875–1920*, vol. 2; a reference to page 25 appears in Moore's notes in the back of the book.

67. Rosenbach Museum and Library, 11fw3.5, Moore's copy of Eliot, *For Lancelot Andrewes*; a reference to page 12 appears in Moore's notes in the back of the book.

68. Rosenbach Museum and Library, Vertical File: Literature A–Z, clipping of Victor Howes, "In Mr. Pope's Grotto."

69. See Rosenbach Museum and Library, VII:05:7, 1251/27, notebook which contains Moore's notes from her English course, "Imitative Writing."

70. Robert Burton, *The Anatomy of Melancholy*, 24–25.

71. Stapleton, *Marianne Moore: The Poet's Advance*, 61.

72. Moore, "Hymen," 133.
73. Williams, "Marianne Moore," 393.

2. "Aristocratic cipher": Moore's Reviews of Stevens

1. Michel Foucault, *The History of Sexuality*, vol. 1, *An Introduction*, 86.
2. *The Letters of Wallace Stevens*, ed. Holly Stevens, no. 328: To Ronald Lane Latimer, p. 290. See also Rosenbach Museum and Library, V:63:22, T.L.S., Wallace Stevens to Marianne Moore, February 3, 1937.
3. See *The Letters of Wallace Stevens*, no. 804: To Herbert Weinstock, pp. 732—33, and no. 806: To Herbert Weinstock, pp. 733—34.
4. Moore, "On Wallace Stevens," 6. Stevens mentions this meeting in a letter to Hi Simons. See *The Letters of Wallace Stevens*, no. 494: To Hi Simons, pp. 457—58.
5. Ibid.
6. Peter Brazeau, *Parts of a World: Wallace Stevens Remembered*, 182.
7. Ibid., 181. He also quotes (p. 184) Constance Saintonge, a Mount Holyoke professor, who reinforces his own sense of Stevens' need for distance: "Stevens made an impression, surely. It was wonderful to have him here. But he was like an angel who flew in for a minute and went out. [I remember] mostly the look of him, the impression as a person in this immaculate pearl-gray suit, looking very smooth and pink above it. And then the three ladies in pastel coats who bore him away afterward the minute it was over. They surrounded him and carried him off to a waiting car. I had the impression that this was to protect his privacy, not to get any more involved."
8. Brazeau quotes (p. 182) Alan McGee, a member of the Mount Holyoke English department, who describes Marianne Moore's presence at the conference: "Marianne Moore and her mother sat there in tricornered hats, looking as much like each other as two women twenty years apart could conceivably look. He was sitting near the porch, and she was right beside him, in the courtyard, facing the audience."
9. Moore, "Unanimity and Fortitude," 268.

10. Moore, "Statements," 31.

11. Moore, "Well Moused, Lion," 84.

12. The phrase "achieved remoteness" appears in "Well Moused, Lion,"
    84. The phrase "method of hints and disguises" appears in "Una-
    nimity and Fortitude," 270.

13. Rosenbach Museum and Library, V:23:32, T.L.C., Marianne Moore
    to H.D., November 10, 1916.

14. She may also have seen his poems which appeared in *Trend* (1914),
    Rogue (1915), and *The Modern School* (1915).

15. At the end of her 1924 review of *Harmonium*, "Well Moused, Lion,"
    Moore mentions poems that Stevens "has been careful to omit from
    his collected work. One regrets, however, the omission by Mr. Ste-
    vens of The Indigo Glass in the Grass, The Man Whose Pharynx Was
    Bad, La Mort du Soldat Est Près des Choses Naturelles (5 Mars) and
    Comme Dieu Dispense de Graces." All of these poems appeared
    between 1918 and 1921 in little magazines, but were not included
    in *Harmonium*.

16. Moore's three essays in *Predilections*, although based on earlier re-
    views, are considered as separate pieces because of her revisions.
    Her reviews of Stevens include "Well Moused, Lion," "Ideas of Or-
    der," "Unanimity and Fortitude," "There Is a War that Never Ends,"
    "The World Imagined . . . Since We Are Poor," "Statements," "A
    Tribute," and "On Wallace Stevens."

17. Rosenbach Museum and Library, V:63:22, T.L.C., Marianne Moore
    to Wallace Stevens, March 10, 1936.

18. Rosenbach Museum and Library, loose notes found in the back of
    Moore's copy of *Harmonium*.

19. Moore, "Statements," 31.

20. Moore, "There Is a War that Never Ends," 144.

21. Moore, "Unanimity and Fortitude," 268.

22. *The Letters of Wallace Stevens*, no. 322: To Ronald Lane Latimer,
    p. 284.

23. Rosenbach Museum and Library, V:17:26, T.L.C., Marianne Moore
    to T. S. Eliot, October 4, 1935.

24. Moore, "Ideas of Order," 309.

25. Rosenbach Museum and Library, V:63:22, T.L.C., Marianne Moore
    to Wallace Stevens, October 29, 1936.

26. Moore, "Unanimity and Fortitude," 272.
27. Moore, "On Wallace Stevens," 5.
28. These phrases appear in "Well Moused, Lion," 87, and "Ideas of Order," 307.
29. Moore, "There Is a War that Never Ends," 146.
30. Rosenbach Museum and Library, V:77:26, T.L.D., Marianne Moore to William Carlos Williams, November 12, 1944.
31. Helen Vendler, *On Extended Wings: Wallace Stevens' Longer Poems*, 207.
32. Moore, "Well Moused, Lion," 86.
33. See Helen Vendler, *Wallace Stevens: Words Chosen Out of Desire*, 10—28.
34. Rosenbach Museum and Library, VII:04:04, 1251/7, Poetry Workbook 1923—30.
35. Bonnie Costello, "Marianne Moore's Debt and Tribute to Wallace Stevens."
36. Ibid., 29.
37. Moore, "Well Moused, Lion," 84.
38. Moore, "Ideas of Order," 308.
39. Ibid.
40. Moore, "Unanimity and Fortitude," 270.
41. See Kermode's discussion of Hermes in Frank Kermode, *The Genesis of Secrecy: On the Interpretation of Narrative*, 1—21.
42. Moore, "A Bold Virtuoso," in *Predilections*, 43.
43. Moore, "Well Moused, Lion," 87.
44. Moore, "Unanimity and Fortitude," 270.
45. Stevens, "Ordinary Evening in New Haven," in *The Palm at the End of the Mind*, ed. Holly Stevens, 337.
46. Ibid.
47. Moore, "Well Moused, Lion," 89.
48. Ibid., 90.
49. W. H. Hudson, *Far Away and Long Ago*, 187.
50. Ibid., 190.
51. Moore, "Well Moused, Lion," 84.
52. Harold Bloom, *Wallace Stevens: The Poems of Our Climate*, 17.
53. My phrase comes from Moore's poem "He 'Digesteth Harde Yron,'" in *The Complete Poems of Marianne Moore*, 99—100.
54. Moore, "Unanimity and Fortitude," 269.

55. Ibid., 271.

56. Rosenbach Museum and Library, Vertical File: Twentieth Century Art. Moore retained the brochure from the Daniel Gallery which announced: "Recent Paintings and Drawings by Yasuo Kuniyoshi, Closing January 22, 1924."

57. See "Well Moused, Lion," 88, where Moore notes: ". . . The Comedian as the Letter C, as the account of the craftsman's un [sic] 'simple jaunt,' is an expanded metaphor which becomes as one contemplates it, hypnotically incandescent like the rose tinged fringe of the night blooming cereus."

58. There is evidence that Moore associated "The Load of Sugar-Cane" with "Peter Quince at the Clavier." See Rosenbach Museum and Library, loose notes found in the back of Moore's copy of *Harmonium* where she notes

      27   The *going* of the glade-boat
            Is like water *flowing*;   cf Peter Quince

59. Ibid. These notes also contain

      31   [The search for
             "A damsel heightened by eternal bloom"
            is profitless—

60. Rosenbach Museum and Library, II:07:02, Unpublished Prose, "Understatement" (ca. 1917–18), 3.

61. Moore seems to have thought of these two images in conjunction with one another. See Rosenbach Museum and Library, loose notes found in the back of Moore's copy of *Harmonium*, where she notes: "cf night blooming cereus spinnaker."

62. Moore, "Comment" (July 1925), 87.

63. Moore, "Ideas of Order," 308.

64. Moore, "Well Moused, Lion," 86.

65. Moore, "'New' Poetry Since 1912," 175–76.

66. Moore, "Unanimity and Fortitude," 271.

67. Moore, "Well Moused, Lion," 84.

68. Moore, "There Is a War that Never Ends," 145.

69. Henry W. and Albert A. Berg Collection, New York Public Library,

Astor, Lenox and Tilden Foundations, A.L.S., Marianne Moore to James Sibley Watson, July 22, 1921.

70. This unpublished letter is cited in Alan Filreis, "Voicing the Desert of Silence: Stevens' Letters to Alice Corbin Henderson," *The Wallace Stevens Journal*, 12 (Spring 1988), 17. In this same letter Stevens also indicates that he does not care for Williams.

71. See Stevens, "A Poet that Matters," and "About One of Marianne Moore's Poems," *Quarterly Review of Literature*, 4, No. 2 (1948), 143–49; rpt. in Stevens, *The Necessary Angel: Essays on Reality and the Imagination*, 93–103.

72. Stevens, "About One of Marianne Moore's Poems," rpt. in Stevens, *The Necessary Angel*, 96.

73. *The Letters of Wallace Stevens*, no. 314: To T. C. Wilson, pp. 278–79.

74. See Rosenbach Museum and Library, V:78:04, T.L.S., T. C. Wilson to Marianne Moore, April 9, 1935.

75. See chapter 4 for a discussion of Moore's criticism of Williams and the role Stevens played in it.

76. Stevens, preface to his *Collected Poems, 1921–1931*, rpt. in *William Carlos Williams: A Critical Anthology*, ed. Tomlinson, 128.

77. *The Letters of Wallace Stevens*, no. 319: To T. C. Wilson, p. 282.

78. Rosenbach Museum and Library, V:63:22, T.L.S., Wallace Stevens to Marianne Moore, March 9, 1936.

79. Stevens, "A Poet that Matters," 62.

80. See *The Letters of Wallace Stevens*, no. 319: To T. C. Wilson, p. 282. Stevens wrote to Wilson: "Both the poem SAILING AFTER LUNCH, and the note on SELECTED POEMS are expressions of the same thing. The poem preceded the note."

81. Stevens, "A Poet that Matters," 63.

3. *"Firm piloting of rebellious fluency"*: Moore's Reviews of Pound's Cantos

1. Rosenbach Museum and Library, V:50:06, T.L.C., Marianne Moore to Ezra Pound, June 19, 1919.

2. Moore, "Comment" (July 1925), 87.

3. Moore, "Comment" (March 1928), 269. See Rosenbach Museum

and Library, no no., 1250/25, Conversation Notebook, for the source of this remark: "E. E. Cummings Nov. 30, 1927 E. Pound He has a fringy mind—that moves back and forth, like seaweed. It's the intuitive or feminine mind if there is such a thing."

4. Moore, "The Cantos," 45.
5. Ibid., 48.
6. Moore, "A Draft of XXX Cantos," 485.
7. Moore, "The Cantos," 42.
8. Ibid., 50.
9. Ibid., 37.
10. See also T. S. Eliot, "The Method of Mr. Pound," 1065. Eliot maintains here that Pound "must hide to reveal himself. But if we collate all these disguises we find not a mere collection of green-room properties, but Mr. Pound."
11. Moore, "A Draft of XXX Cantos," 482.
12. Moore, "The Cantos," 47. I am quoting Moore who is quoting Pound on James.
13. Although Moore referred briefly to Pound throughout the twenties in "Comments" written for *The Dial* and in "'New' Poetry Since 1912," she did not write a full-length review of his work until 1931 when she reviewed *A Draft of XXX Cantos* for *Poetry*.
14. Patricia C. Willis, "Marianne Moore on Ezra Pound 1909–1915."
15. See Rosenbach Museum and Library, Moore's copies of BAB 3/49, *Personae*; BAB 3/45, *Exultations*; BAB 3/39, *Canzoni*; BAB 3/47, *Lustra of Ezra Pound with Earlier Poems*; BAB 3/51, *Pavannes and Divisions*; BAB 3/50, *Instigations*; no no., *Indiscretions*; and GBW2L/27, *Antheil and the Treatise on Harmony*.
16. See Pound, "Marianne Moore and Mina Loy."
17. See *The Selected Letters of Ezra Pound 1907–1941*, ed. D. D. Paige, no. 155: To Marianne Moore, pp. 141–44, and no. 179: To Marianne Moore, pp. 167–68.
18. The *Dial* correspondence housed at the Beinecke Library at Yale University includes Moore's letters to and from Pound between 1925 and 1929.
19. There was some suggestion made that Pound receive the *Dial* Award for his prose. Pound wrote to J. S. Watson, indicating that this would

be impossible. See *The Selected Letters of Ezra Pound 1907–1941*, no. 226: To James S. Watson, Jr., p. 213.

20. See Rosenbach Museum and Library, V:49:14, A.L.S., Harriet Monroe to Marianne Moore, September 2, 1931.

21. Yeats, "Ezra Pound," from the introduction to *The Oxford Book of Modern Verse*, ed. Yeats; rpt. in Walter Sutton, ed., *Ezra Pound: A Collection of Critical Essays*, 9–10.

22. *The Selected Letters of Ezra Pound*, no. 355: To Hubert Creekmore, p. 321.

23. See Sutton's introduction to *Ezra Pound: A Collection of Critical Essays*, 3. For two other typical British reactions to the *Cantos*, see H. B. Parkes, "Two Pounds of Poetry," rpt. in Eric Homberger, ed., *Ezra Pound: The Critical Heritage*, 239–45; Geoffrey Grigson, "The Methodism of Ezra Pound," rpt. in Homberger, ed., *Ezra Pound: The Critical Heritage*, 259–64.

24. See Ronald Bush, *The Genesis of Ezra Pound's Cantos*, 5–6: "Reviewing the *Cantos*, Maxwell Bodenheim, Babette Deutsch, Delmore Schwartz, Allen Tate, and R. P. Blackmur, among others, put the unity of the poem in the character of Pound's mind." Bush might also have included Moore in his list.

25. *The Selected Letters of Ezra Pound*, no. 355: To Hubert Creekmore, p. 321.

26. Williams, "Marianne Moore," 393.

27. Ibid., 395.

28. Williams, "Excerpts from a Critical Sketch: *A Draft of XXX Cantos* by Ezra Pound," rpt. in Sutton, ed., *Ezra Pound: A Collection of Critical Essays*, 15.

29. For a good discussion of Williams' relationship with Pound and Eliot, see Geoffrey Movius, " 'Two halves of . . . a fairly decent poet': William Carlos Williams and Ezra Pound 1914–1920."

30. Moore, "The Cantos," 43–44.

31. Ibid., 43.

32. Beinecke Library, T.L.S., Marianne Moore to William Carlos Williams, September 18, 1931.

33. See Rosenbach Museum and Library, II:01:23, 48 pages of manuscript notes for "The Cantos."

34. Eliot, "Ezra Pound," 335. "I have already said," Eliot asserts, "that Pound's criticism would not have the great value it has, without his poetry; and in his poetry there is, for the analytical reader, a great deal of criticism exemplified." See also Kenner, *The Poetry of Ezra Pound*.

35. Moore, "The Cantos," 46–47.

36. Eliot, *The Sacred Wood*, 16.

37. Kenner, *The Poetry of Ezra Pound*, 34.

38. See Rosenbach Museum and Library, II:01:23, 48 pages of manuscript notes for "The Cantos." We find references to Eliot's "Isolated Superiority," which appeared in *The Dial* in 1928, and to "Ezra Pound: His Metric and Poetry," which appeared anonymously in 1918.

39. See Rosenbach Museum and Library, BAB 3/49, Moore's copy of *Personae*.

40. See Eliot, "The Method of Mr. Pound," and Pound, "To the Editor of *The Athenaeum*."

41. Eliot, "The Method of Mr. Pound," 1065.

42. Ibid. See also Eliot's introduction to *Selected Poems*, by Ezra Pound, xii: "Now Mr. Pound is often most 'original' in the right sense, when he is most 'archaeological' in the ordinary sense."

43. Moore, "The Cantos," 42.

44. Eliot, "The Method of Mr. Pound," 1065.

45. Eliot, "A Note on Ezra Pound," 7.

46. Eliot, "Ezra Pound: His Metric and Poetry," 182.

47. See Rosenbach Museum and Library, II:01:23, 48 pages of manuscript notes for "The Cantos." For a history of Eliot's essay and Pound's contribution to it, see Donald Gallup, *T. S. Eliot: A Bibliography*, rev. and extended ed. (New York: Harcourt Brace and World, 1969), 24.

48. Moore, "The Cantos," 45.

49. Eliot, "Ezra Pound: His Metric and Poetry," 171–72.

50. Rosenbach Museum and Library, II:01:23, manuscript notes for "The Cantos."

51. Moore, "The Cantos," 48.

52. Moore, "A Draft of XXX Cantos," 484.

53. Moore, *Predilections*, 10.
54. Moore, "The Cantos," 49.
55. Curt Sachs, *World History of the Dance*, 283.
56. Moore, "The Cantos," 47–48.
57. Pound, *Literary Essays of Ezra Pound*, 321. We know from Moore's manuscript notes for her 1931 review of the *Cantos* that she had read this essay in Pound's *Instigations* (1920).
58. Pound, *Pavannes and Divisions*, 234.
59. Moore cites this passage in her manuscript notes for "The Cantos":

> 234   Poetry is a centaur—the thinking word-
>   arranging, clarifying must move + leap
>   w the energizing sentient, musical
>   faculty.

60. Moore, "A Draft of XXX Cantos," 484.
61. Ibid., 483.
62. Ibid., 482.
63. Ibid.
64. Tate, "Ezra Pound's Golden Ass," 632–33.
65. Pound, *ABC of Reading*, 18. See also Ian F. A. Bell, *Critic as Scientist: The Modernist Poetics of Ezra Pound*, and Hugh Kenner, *The Pound Era*.
66. Pound, *ABC of Reading*, 17–18.

4. *"Poets are never of the world in which they live": Moore's Quarrel with Williams*

1. Rosenbach Museum and Library, V:50:07, T.L.C., Marianne Moore to Ezra Pound, February 16, 1934.
2. Williams, *I Wanted to Write a Poem: The Autobiography of the Works of a Poet*, 79–80.
3. Ibid., 79.
4. Randall Jarrell, "A View of Three Poets," 698.
5. Randall Jarrell, "The Poet and His Public," 493.
6. Ibid., 498.
7. Paul Mariani, *William Carlos Williams: A New World Naked*, 585. Mariani maintains that "the Introduction here served as a halfway

house between the praise of *Paterson* I (1946) and the disenchant-ment of Jarrell's essay five years later."

8. Randall Jarrell, "An Introduction to the *Selected Poems of William Car-los Williams*," rpt. in Jarrell, *Poetry and the Age*, 238–39.

9. Williams quotes a letter he supposedly received from Stevens in his prologue to *Kora in Hell*, rpt. in *Imaginations*, ed. Webster Schott (New York: New Directions Publishing Corp., 1970), 15. See also Bonnie Costello, "'Polished Garlands' of Agreeing Difference: Wil-liam Carlos Williams and Marianne Moore, an Exchange," 64–81. Costello traces the "growing rift over fundamental questions of style and decorum" (p. 64) between Moore and Williams as exemplified in some of their correspondence and in their reviews of one another, but is finally interested in establishing that in their poetry "they worked at cross-purposes, though often with similar results" (p. 65).

10. Rosenbach Museum and Library, V:44:3, T.L.C., Marianne Moore to Barbara Asch, May 22, 1951.

11. Rosenbach Museum and Library, V:77:26, T.L.S., William Carlos Williams to Marianne Moore, June 19, 1951.

12. Rosenbach Museum and Library, V:77:26, T.L.C., Marianne Moore to William Carlos Williams, June 22, 1951.

13. Williams, *I Wanted to Write a Poem*, 80.

14. When Eliot wrote the introduction for her *Selected Poems* in 1935, Moore thanked him for the armor it had provided. See Rosenbach Museum and Library, V:17:26, T.L.C., Marianne Moore to T. S. Eliot, June 27, 1935.

15. Stevens, "Preface to *Collected Poems: 1921–1931*,"; rpt. in *William Carlos Williams: A Critical Anthology*, ed. Charles Tomlinson, 129.

16. See Rosenbach Museum and Library, V:77:25, T.L.S., William Car-los Williams to Marianne Moore, May 9, 1916.

17. Rosenbach Museum and Library, V:23:32, T.L.C., Marianne Moore to H.D., November 10, 1916.

18. Mariani, *William Carlos Williams: A New World Naked*, 144.

19. Rosenbach Museum and Library, V:77:25, A.L.D., Marianne Moore to William Carlos Williams, February 23, 1917.

20. See Rosenbach Museum and Library, V:23:32, T.L.C., Marianne Moore to H.D., March 27, 1921.

21. Rosenbach Museum and Library, V:77:25, T.L.S., William Carlos Williams to Marianne Moore, December, n.d., 1923.
22. Mariani, *William Carlos Williams: A New World Naked*, 216–17.
23. Rosenbach Museum and Library, V:77:25, T.L.S., William Carlos Williams to Marianne Moore, February 10, 1924.
24. Rosenbach Museum and Library, V:23:32, T.L.C., Marianne Moore to H.D., March 27, 1921.
25. Rosenbach Museum and Library, V:77:25, T.L.S., William Carlos Williams to Marianne Moore, May 23, 1921.
26. Moore, "*Kora in Hell* by William Carlos Williams," *Contact*, 7.
27. Ibid.
28. Ibid., 5.
29. Ibid.
30. Rosenbach Museum and Library, V:77:25, A.L.S., Marianne Moore to William Carlos Williams, April 16, 1917.
31. Moore, "*Kora in Hell* by Williams Carlos Williams," 6.
32. Ibid., 5.
33. Williams, *Kora in Hell*; rpt. in Schott, *Imaginations*, 35.
34. Moore, "*Kora in Hell* by William Carlos Williams," 7.
35. Moore, "Briefer Mention of *In the American Grain*."
36. See Rosenbach Museum and Library, V:75:02, A.L.S., James Sibley Watson to Marianne Moore, October 10, 1925, and A.L.S., James Sibley Watson to Marianne Moore, November 7, 1925.
37. Moore, "Announcement," 88.
38. Ibid., 89.
39. Ibid.
40. Ibid.
41. Ibid., 88.
42. *The Letters of Wallace Stevens*, no. 270: To Marianne Moore, p. 246.
43. Ibid., no. 273: To Marianne Moore, p. 248.
44. See Moore's copy of *Kora in Hell* (Rosenbach Museum and Library, LRF41). In the back she makes one reference to Williams' prologue; she refers to Stevens' letter about Williams' poems, which Williams reprinted in his prologue.
45. Mariani, *William Carlos Williams: The Poet and His Critics*, 45. He maintains: "Marianne Moore's review, 'Things Others Never Notice,' . . . considered Williams in the light of Stevens' prefatory remarks."

46. Williams, *I Wanted to Write a Poem*, 52.
47. *The Letters of Wallace Stevens*, no. 314: To T. C. Wilson, pp. 278–79.
48. Stevens, preface to Williams, *Collected Poems: 1921–1931*, 128.
49. Ibid., 129.
50. Moore, "Things Others Never Notice," 105.
51. Ibid.
52. Moore, "A Poet of the Quattrocento," 215.
53. Moore, "Things Others Never Notice," 106.
54. Stevens, preface to Williams, *Collected Poems: 1921–1931*, 129.
55. Moore, "Things Others Never Notice," 103.
56. Gelpi, "Stevens and Williams: The Epistemology of Modernism," 10–11.
57. Moore, "Things Others Never Notice," 105.
58. Rosenbach Museum and Library, V:35:22, T.L.C., Marianne Moore to Ronald Lane Latimer, October 7, 1935.
59. Rosenbach Museum and Library, V:77:25, T.L.C., Marianne Moore to William Carlos Williams, October 17, 1935.
60. Rosenbach Museum and Library, V:77:25, T.L.S., William Carlos Williams to Marianne Moore, October 18, 1935.
61. Rosenbach Museum and Library, V:77:26, T.L.C., Marianne Moore to William Carlos Williams, December 7, 1936.
62. Moore, "A Vein of Anthracite."
63. Rosenbach Museum and Library, V:77:26, T.L.S., William Carlos Williams to Marianne Moore, December 23, 1936.
64. Rosenbach Museum and Library, V:77:26, T.L.C., Marianne Moore to William Carlos Williams, December 24, 1936.
65. Mariani, *William Carlos Williams: A New World Naked*, 393.
66. Moore, "A Vein of Anthracite."
67. Ibid.
68. Rosenbach Museum and Library, VII:04:03, 1251/1, Conversation Notebook, 1935–1947.
69. Moore, "A Vein of Anthracite."
70. Rosenbach Museum and Library, V:77:26, T.L.C., Marianne Moore to William Carlos Williams, January 7, 1941.
71. *The Letters of Wallace Stevens*, no. 592: To José Rodríguez Feo, p. 544.

5. "Combative sincerity" and "Studious constraint": The Literary Exchanges of Moore and Eliot

1. T. S. Eliot, introduction to *The Art of Poetry*, by Paul Valery, vii. Moore marked this passage in her copy of this book.
2. Rosenbach Museum and Library, V:18:04, T.L.S., T. S. Eliot to Marianne Moore, October 24, 1956.
3. Rosenbach Museum and Library, V:17:26, T.L.S., T. S. Eliot to Marianne Moore, September 20, 1935.
4. Rosenbach Museum and Library, V:17:26, T.L.C., Marianne Moore to T. S. Eliot, October 4, 1935.
5. See Rosenbach Museum and Library, V:17:24, A.L.S., T. S. Eliot to Marianne Moore, April 3, 1921.
6. Rosenbach Museum and Library, V:17:24, A.L.S., Marianne Moore to T. S. Eliot, April 17, 1921.
7. Geoffrey H. Hartman, *Criticism in the Wilderness: The Study of Literature Today*, 36.
8. Rosenbach Museum and Library, V:17:24, A.D. Unsigned, Marianne Moore to T. S. Eliot, July 15, 1921.
9. Ibid.
10. Rosenbach Museum and Library, V:17:24, A.D. Unsigned, Marianne Moore to T. S. Eliot, May 3, 1925.
11. Rosenbach Museum and Library, V:17:25, T.L.C., Marianne Moore to T. S. Eliot, March 15, 1934.
12. Rosenbach Museum and Library, Moore's copies of Eliot's books: 11fw3'31, *The Sacred Wood*; 11fw3'5, *For Lancelot Andrewes*; 11fw3'2, *The Use of Poetry and the Use of Criticism*; BAB 3/8, *Notes toward the Definition of Culture*; 11fw3'13, *Selected Essays*; and GB 70, *Poetry and Drama*.
13. Rosenbach Museum and Library, V:17:25, T.L.C., Marianne Moore to T. S. Eliot, June 16, 1934.
14. See Rosenbach Museum and Library, II:01:23, 48 pages of manuscript notes for "The Cantos."
15. Rosenbach Museum and Library, V:17:26, T.L.S., Marianne Moore to T. S. Eliot, November 4, 1946.
16. See Rosenbach Museum and Library, V:17:24, A.D., Marianne Moore to T. S. Eliot, December 25, 1933.

17. See Rosenbach Museum and Library, V:17:24, T.L.S., T. S. Eliot to Marianne Moore, December 10, 1931; Rosenbach Museum and Library, V:17:24, T.L.S., T. S. Eliot to Marianne Moore, December 8, 1933; Rosenbach Museum and Library, V:17:25, T.L.C., Marianne Moore to T. S. Eliot, February 28, 1934.

18. See Rosenbach Museum and Library, V:18:04, T.L.S., T. S. Eliot to Marianne Moore, October 24, 1956.

19. Rosenbach Museum and Library, V:17:24, A.L.S., T. S. Eliot to Marianne Moore, October 4, 1923.

20. Eliot, "Marianne Moore," rpt. in *Marianne Moore: A Collection of Critical Essays*, ed. Charles Tomlinson, 49.

21. Ibid.

22. See Williams, "Marianne Moore."

23. Eliot, introduction to *Selected Poems*, by Marianne Moore (New York: Macmillan, 1935; London: Faber and Faber, 1935); rpt. in Tomlinson, *Marianne Moore: A Collection of Critical Essays*, 62.

24. Rosenbach Museum and Library, V:17:24, A.D. Unsigned, Marianne Moore to T. S. Eliot, December 10, 1923.

25. Ibid.

26. Rosenbach Museum and Library, V:17:26, T.L.C., Marianne Moore to T. S. Eliot, June 27, 1935.

27. Eliot, introduction to *Selected Poems*, by Marianne Moore; rpt. in Tomlinson, *Marianne Moore: A Collection of Critical Essays*, 61.

28. Rosenbach Museum and Library, V:17:25, T.L.C., Marianne Moore to T. S. Eliot, October 23, 1934.

29. Ibid.

30. See, for example, R. P. Blackmur, "The Method of Marianne Moore," in *The Double Agent: Essays in Craft and Elucidation*, by R. P. Blackmur, 141–71; and Randall Jarrell, "Her Shield," in *Poetry and the Age* (1953); rpt. in Tomlinson, *Marianne Moore: A Collection of Critical Essays*, 114–24.

31. Eliot, introduction to *Selected Poems*, by Marianne Moore; rpt. in Tomlinson, *Marianne Moore: A Collection of Critical Essays*, 62.

32. Ibid.

33. Ibid., 63.

34. Rosenbach Museum and Library, V:17:25, T.L.S., T. S. Eliot to Marianne Moore, January 5, 1934.

35. Rosenbach Museum and Library, V:17:25, T.L.C., Marianne Moore to T. S. Eliot, January 18, 1934.
36. Rosenbach Museum and Library, V:17:25, T.L.S., T. S. Eliot to Marianne Moore, January 31, 1934.
37. See Rosenbach Museum and Library, V:17:25, T.L.S., T. S. Eliot to Marianne Moore, April 12, 1934, and Huntington Library, A.L.S., Marianne Moore to Wallace Stevens, July 11, 1935.
38. Rosenbach Museum and Library, V:17:25, T.L.S., T. S. Eliot to Marianne Moore, April 12, 1934.
39. Rosenbach Museum and Library, V:17:25, T.L.C., Marianne Moore to T. S. Eliot, April 18, 1934.
40. See Rosenbach Museum and Library, V:17:25, T.L.C., Marianne Moore to T. S. Eliot, May 16, 1934.
41. Rosenbach Museum and Library, V:17:25, T.L.S., T. S. Eliot to Marianne Moore, June 20, 1934.
42. Rosenbach Museum and Library, V:17:25, T.L.C., Marianne Moore to T. S. Eliot, July 2, 1934.
43. Ibid.
44. Rosenbach Museum and Library, V:17:25, T.L.C., Marianne Moore to T. S. Eliot, October 23, 1934.
45. See Rosenbach Museum and Library, V:17:26, T.L.S., T. S. Eliot to Marianne Moore, September 20, 1935.
46. Rosenbach Museum and Library, V:17:25, T.L.C., Marianne Moore to T. S. Eliot, October 23, 1934.
47. Rosenbach Museum and Library, V:17:25, T.L.S., T. S. Eliot to Marianne Moore, June 28, 1934.
48. Rosenbach Museum and Library, V:17:25, T.L.S., T. S. Eliot to Marianne Moore, October 5, 1934.
49. Rosenbach Museum and Library, V:17:25, T.L.S., T. S. Eliot to Marianne Moore, October 31, 1934.
50. Rosenbach Museum and Library, V:18:02, T.L.S., T. S. Eliot to Marianne Moore, July 31, 1950.
51. Rosenbach Museum and Library, V:18:02, T.L.C., Marianne Moore to T. S. Eliot, August 4, 1950.
52. Rosenbach Museum and Library, V:17:24, T.L.C., Marianne Moore to T. S. Eliot, December 24, 1931.
53. Moore, "There Is a War that Never Ends," 146.

54. Moore, *"Ideas of Order,"* 309.

55. "A Note on T. S. Eliot's Book" (1918); "The Sacred Wood" (1921); "A Machinery of Satisfaction" (1931); "Sweeney Agonistes" (1933); "If I Am Worthy There Is No Danger" (1936); "It Is Not Forbidden to Think" (1936); and "Reticent Candor," in *Predilections* (1955), 52–61.

56. Moore, "A Note on T. S. Eliot's Book," 36.

57. Pound, "Drunken Helots and Mr. Eliot," 72–73.

58. Moore, "A Note on T. S. Eliot's Book," 37.

59. Pound, "T. S. Eliot," *Poetry*, 10 (August 1917), 267.

60. Ibid., 266–67.

61. Rosenbach Museum and Library, V:17:24, A.L.S., Marianne Moore to T. S. Eliot, April 17, 1921.

62. Moore, "The Sacred Wood," 336.

63. Eliot, *The Sacred Wood: Essays on Poetry and Criticism*, 16.

64. Ibid., 17.

65. Ibid., 19.

66. Ibid.

67. Moore, "The Sacred Wood," 336.

68. Ibid., 339.

69. Ibid., 336.

70. Ibid.

71. Eliot, *The Sacred Wood*, 144.

72. Ibid., 148.

73. Moore, "The Sacred Wood," 337.

74. Ibid.

75. Ibid., 339.

76. Ackroyd, *T. S. Eliot: A Life*, 88.

77. Moore, unpublished prose, "English Literature Since 1914" (1920); rpt. from Moore's carbon copy in the *Marianne Moore Newsletter*, 4 (Fall 1980), 21.

78. Significant critical commentary has since been devoted to the mutual influences between their work. See Abbie F. Willard, *Wallace Stevens: The Poet and His Critics*, 105–10.

79. Rosenbach Museum and Library, VII:01:03, 1250/3, Reading Notebook 1921–22, 43.

80. Rosenbach Museum and Library, LLF 2/4, Moore's copy of *Harmonium*.
81. Moore, "Unanimity and Fortitude," 269–70.
82. Moore, "A Machinery of Satisfaction," 337.
83. Ibid., 338.
84. Ibid.
85. Ibid., 338–39.
86. Ibid., 339.
87. Rosenbach Museum and Library, V:17:25, T.L.C., Marianne Moore to T. S. Eliot, June 16, 1934.
88. Moore, "It Is Not Forbidden to Think," 681.
89. Ibid., 680.
90. Moore, "Comment" (February 1926), 178.
91. Moore, "It Is Not Forbidden to Think," 680.
92. Ibid., 681.
93. Moore, *Predilections*, 53.
94. Ibid., 52.

Afterword

1. Moore, "Idiosyncrasy and Technique," in *A Marianne Moore Reader*, 171.
2. R. P. Blackmur, "The Method of Marianne Moore," in Blackmur, *The Double Agent: Essays in Craft and Elucidation*, 141.
3. Gerald L. Bruns, "De Improvisatione," 67.
4. Ibid., 68.
5. Ibid., 69.
6. Ibid., 70.
7. Williams, "Marianne Moore," 393; rpt. in *Marianne Moore: A Collection of Critical Essays*, ed. Charles Tomlinson, 52.
8. Ibid.
9. Eliot, introduction to *Selected Poems*; rpt. in *Marianne Moore: A Collection of Critical Essays*, 62.
10. Ibid.
11. Harold Bloom, *Wallace Stevens: The Poems of Our Climate*, 152. In "The Creations of Sound" Stevens indicts an unnamed poet because "his poems are not of the second part of life. / They do not make

the visible a little hard / To see. . . ." Bloom suggests that this poet may be T. S. Eliot.

12. Stevens, "Someone Puts a Pineapple Together," in Stevens, *The Palm at the End of the Mind: Selected Poems and a Play*, 299.

13. Stevens, "A Poet that Matters," 63.

14. Blackmur, "Masks of Ezra Pound," in *The Double Agent*, 31.

15. Ibid.

16. Ibid., 45.

17. Blackmur, "Examples of Wallace Stevens," in *The Double Agent*, 89.

18. Ibid.

19. Blackmur, "Masks of Ezra Pound," in *The Double Agent*, 49.

20. Moore, "*Kora in Hell* by William Carlos Williams," 5.

21. Ibid.

22. Ibid., 7.

23. Moore, "Things Others Never Notice," 105.

24. See Rosenbach Museum and Library, V:77:26, T.L.D., Marianne Moore to William Carlos Williams, November 12, 1944.

Selected Bibliography

Ackroyd, Peter. *T. S. Eliot: A Life*. New York: Simon and Schuster, 1984.

Bell, Ian F. A. *Critic as Scientist: The Modernist Poetics of Ezra Pound*. London and New York: Methuen and Company, 1981.

Blackmur, R. P. *The Double Agent: Essays in Craft and Elucidation*. 1935; rpt. Gloucester, Mass.: Peter Smith, 1962.

————. *Language as Gesture: Essays in Poetry*. 1952; rpt. New York: Columbia University Press, 1981.

Bloom, Harold, ed. *Selected Writings of Walter Pater*. New York: New American Library, 1974.

————. *Wallace Stevens: The Poems of Our Climate*. Ithaca and London: Cornell University Press, 1977.

Bogan, Louise. "Predilections." *New Yorker*, 21 (30 July 1955), 67–68.

Brazeau, Peter. *Parts of a World: Wallace Stevens Remembered*. San Francisco: North Point Press, 1985.

Brown, Ashley, and Robert S. Haller, eds. *The Achievement of Wallace Stevens*. New York: Lippincott Company, 1962.

Bruns, Gerald L. "De Improvisatione." *Iowa Review*, 9, No. 3 (Summer 1978), 66–78.

Burke, Kenneth. "Likings of an Observationalist." *Poetry*, 87 (January 1956), 239–47. Rpt. in *Marianne Moore: A Collection of Critical Essays*, ed. Charles Tomlinson. Englewood Cliffs, N.J.: Prentice-Hall, 1969.

Burton, Robert. *The Anatomy of Melancholy*. Ed. Holbrook Jackson. 1932; rpt. New York: Vintage Books, 1977.

Bush, Ronald. *The Genesis of Ezra Pound's Cantos*. Princeton: Princeton University Press, 1976.

Costello, Bonnie. *Marianne Moore: Imaginary Possessions*. Cambridge: Harvard University Press, 1981.

————. "Marianne Moore's Debt and Tribute to Wallace Stevens." *Concerning Poetry*, 15, No. 1 (Spring 1982), 27–33.

―――. "'Polished Garlands' of Agreeing Difference: William Carlos Williams and Marianne Moore, an Exchange." In *The Motive for Metaphor: Essays on Modern Poetry*, ed. Francis C. Blessington and Guy Rotella. Boston: Northeastern University Press, 1983.

―――. "Marianne Moore and Elizabeth Bishop: Friendship and Influence." *Twentieth Century Literature*, 30 (Summer/Fall 1984), 130−49.

Ehrenpreis, Irvin, ed. *Wallace Stevens: A Critical Anthology*. Middlesex, England: Penguin Books, 1972.

Eisenstein, Hester, and Alice Jardine, eds. *The Future of Difference*. Boston: G. K. Hall and Company, 1980.

Eliot, T. S. "A Note on Ezra Pound." *To-day*, 4, 19 (September 1918), 3−9.

―――. "The Method of Mr. Pound." *The Athenaeum*, October 24, 1919, 1065−66.

―――. *The Sacred Wood: Essays on Poetry and Criticism*. 1920; rpt. London: Methuen and Company, 1960.

―――. "Marianne Moore." *The Dial*, 75 (December 1923), 594−97. Rpt. in *Marianne Moore: A Collection of Critical Essays*, ed. Charles Tomlinson. Englewood Cliffs, N.J.: Prentice-Hall, 1969.

―――. *Poems 1901−1925*. London: Faber and Gwyer, 1926.

―――. *For Lancelot Andrewes*. Garden City, N.Y.: Doubleday, Doran and Company, 1929.

―――. Introduction to *Selected Poems*, by Ezra Pound. London: Faber and Faber, 1933.

―――. *The Use of Poetry and the Use of Criticism*. Cambridge: Harvard University Press, 1933.

―――. Introduction to *Selected Poems*, by Marianne Moore. London: Faber and Faber, 1935.

―――. *Murder in the Cathedral*. London: Faber and Faber, 1935.

―――. *The Family Reunion*. New York: Harcourt, Brace and Company, 1939.

―――. *The Idea of a Christian Society*. New York: Harcourt, Brace and Company, 1940.

―――. "Ezra Pound." *Poetry*, 68 (September 1946), 326−38.

―――. *From Poe to Valery*. New York: Harcourt, Brace and Company, 1948.

———. *Notes toward the Definition of Culture*. London: Faber and Faber, 1948.

———. *Selected Essays*. New York: Harcourt, Brace and Company, 1950.

———. *The Cocktail Party*. London: Faber and Faber, 1950.

———. *Poetry and Drama*. Cambridge: Harvard University Press, 1951.

———. *The Confidential Clerk*. London: Faber and Faber, 1954.

———. *On Poetry and Poets*. New York: Farrar, Straus and Cudahy, 1957.

———. Introduction to *The Art of Poetry*, by Paul Valery. New York: Pantheon Books, 1958.

———. *The Elder Statesman*. New York: Farrar, Straus and Cudahy, 1959.

———. "Ezra Pound: His Metric and Poetry." In *To Criticize the Critic*, by T. S. Eliot. New York: Farrar, Straus and Giroux, 1965.

———. *To Criticize the Critic*. New York: Farrar, Straus and Giroux, 1965.

———. *The Complete Poems and Plays: 1909–1950*. New York: Harcourt Brace and World, 1971.

———. *The Selected Prose of T. S. Eliot*. Ed. and sel. Frank Kermode. New York: Harcourt Brace Jovanovich, 1975.

Engel, Bernard F. *Marianne Moore*. New York: Twayne Publishers, 1964.

Foucault, Michel. *The History of Sexuality*. Vol. 1, *An Introduction*. Trans. Robert Hurley. New York: Vintage Books, 1980.

Fredman, Stephen. *Poet's Prose: The Crisis in American Verse*. London: Cambridge University Press, 1983.

Gelpi, Albert. "Stevens and Williams: The Epistemology of Modernism." In *Wallace Stevens: The Poetics of Modernism*, ed. Albert Gelpi. Cambridge: Cambridge University Press, 1985.

Goodridge, Celeste. "Towards a Poetics of Disclosure: Marianne Moore and Henry James." *Sagetrieb*, 6, no. 3 (Winter 1987), 31–43.

Grant, Michael, ed. *T. S. Eliot: The Critical Heritage*. 2 vols. London and Boston: Routledge and Kegan Paul, 1982.

Grigson, Geoffrey. "The Methodism of Ezra Pound." *New Verse* (October 1933), 17–22. Rpt. in *Ezra Pound: The Critical Heritage*, ed. Eric Homberger. London and Boston: Routledge and Kegan Paul, 1972.

Hall, Donald. *Marianne Moore: The Cage and the Animal*. New York: Western Publishing Co., 1970.

Hartman, Geoffrey. *Criticism in the Wilderness: The Study of Literature Today*. New Haven and London: Yale University Press, 1980.

————. *Saving the Text: Literature/Derrida/Philosophy*. Baltimore and London: Johns Hopkins University Press, 1981.

Holley, Margaret. *The Poetry of Marianne Moore: A Study in Voice and Value*. Cambridge: Cambridge University Press, 1987.

Homberger, Eric, ed. *Ezra Pound: The Critical Heritage*. London and Boston: Routledge and Kegan Paul, 1972.

Howarth, Herbert. *Notes on Some Figures Behind T. S. Eliot*. Boston: Houghton Mifflin Company, 1964.

Howes, Victor. "In Mr. Pope's Grotto." *Christian Science Monitor*, December 29, 1962, 8.

Hudson, W. H. *Far Away and Long Ago*. 1918; rpt. London: J. M. Dent & Sons, 1940.

Jarrell, Randall. "The Poet and His Public." *Partisan Review*, 13 (1946), 488–99.

————. "A View of Three Poets." *Partisan Review*, 18 (1951), 691–700.

————. "An Introduction to the *Selected Poems of William Carlos Williams*." In Jarrell, *Poetry and the Age*, 1953; rpt. New York: Ecco Press, 1980.

————. "Her Shield." In Jarrell, *Poetry and the Age*, 1953; rpt. New York: Ecco Press, 1980. Rpt. in *Marianne Moore: A Collection of Critical Essays*, ed. Charles Tomlinson. Englewood Cliffs, N.J.: Prentice-Hall, 1969.

————. *Kipling, Auden & Co.: Essays and Reviews 1935–1964*. New York: Farrar, Straus and Giroux, 1980.

Joost, Nicholas. *Scofield Thayer and The Dial: An Illustrated History*. Carbondale, Ill.: Southern Illinois University Press, 1964.

Kalstone, David. *Five Temperaments: Elizabeth Bishop, Robert Lowell, James Merrill, Adrienne Rich, John Ashbery*. New York: Oxford University Press, 1977.

————. "Trial Balances: Elizabeth Bishop and Marianne Moore." *Grand Street*, 3 (Autumn 1983), 115–35.

Kearns, George. *Guide to Ezra Pound's Selected Cantos*. New Brunswick, N.J.: Rutgers University Press, 1980.

Keller, Lynn. "Words Worth a Thousand Postcards: The Bishop/Moore Correspondence." *American Literature*, 55 (October 1983), 405–29.

Kenner, Hugh. *The Poetry of Ezra Pound*. 1951; rpt. New York: Kraus Reprint Company, 1968.

————. *The Pound Era*. Berkeley and Los Angeles: University of California Press, 1971.

Kermode, Frank. *Wallace Stevens*. New York: Chip's Bookshop, 1960.

―――. *The Genesis of Secrecy: On the Interpretation of Narrative*. Cambridge and London: Harvard University Press, 1979.

McConnell-Ginet, Sally, Ruth Borker, and Nelly Furman, eds. *Women and Language in Literature and Society*. New York: Praeger, 1980.

Mariani, Paul. *William Carlos Williams: The Poet and His Critics*. Chicago: American Library Association, 1975.

―――. *William Carlos Williams: A New World Naked*. New York: McGraw-Hill, 1981.

Martin, Taffy. "Preparation and Enactment: Marianne Moore's Editorship of *The Dial*." Dissertation, Temple University, 1979.

―――. *Marianne Moore: Subversive Modernist*. Austin, Tex.: University of Texas Press, 1986.

Matthiessen, F. O. *The Achievement of T. S. Eliot*. Boston: Houghton Mifflin Company, 1935.

Monroe, Harriet. "Symposium on Marianne Moore." *Poetry*, 19 (January 1922), 208–16.

Moore, Marianne. "Samuel Butler." *The Chimaera*, 1 (July 1916), 55–56.

―――. "The Accented Syllable." *Egoist*, 3 (October 1916), 151–52.

―――. "A Note on T. S. Eliot's Book." *Poetry*, 12 (April 1918), 36–37.

―――. "Jean de Bosschère's Poems." *Poetry*, 12 (April 1918), 48–51.

―――. "Wild Swans." *Poetry*, 13 (October 1918), 42–44.

―――. "*The Sacred Wood*." *The Dial*, 70 (March 1921), 336–39.

―――. "*Kora in Hell* by William Carlos Williams." *Contact*, No. 4 (Summer 1921), 5–8.

―――. "Hymen." *Broom*, 4 (January 1923), 133–35.

―――. "Well Moused, Lion." *The Dial*, 76 (January 1924), 84–91.

―――. "Comment." *The Dial*, 79 (July 1925), 87–88.

―――. "The Bright Immortal Olive." *The Dial*, 79 (August 1925), 170–72.

―――. "'New' Poetry Since 1912." In *Anthology of Magazine Verse for 1926*, ed. William Stanley Braithwaite. Boston: B. J. Brimmer Company, 1926.

―――. "Comment." *The Dial*, 80 (February 1926), 176–78.

―――. "Briefer Mention of *In the American Grain*." *The Dial*, 80 (March 1926), 253.

―――. "Announcement." *The Dial*, 82 (January 1927), 88–90.

————. "A Poet of the Quattrocento." *The Dial*, 82 (March 1927), 213–15.

————. "Comment." *The Dial*, 84 (March 1928), 268–70.

————. "A Machinery of Satisfaction." *Poetry*, 38 (September 1931), 337–39.

————. "The Cantos." *Poetry*, 39 (October 1931), 37–50.

————. "Sweeney Agonistes." *Poetry*, 42 (May 1933), 106–9.

————. "The Poem and the Print." *Poetry*, 43 (November 1933), 92–95.

————. "A Draft of XXX Cantos." *The Criterion*, 13 (April 1934), 482–85.

————. "Things Others Never Notice." *Poetry*, 44 (May 1934), 103–6.

————. "Archaically New." In *Trial Balances*, ed. Ann Winslow. New York: Macmillan, 1935.

————. "Ideas of Order." *The Criterion*, 15 (January 1936), 307–9.

————. "If I Am Worthy There Is No Danger." *Poetry*, 47 (February 1936), 279–81.

————. "It Is Not Forbidden to Think." *Nation*, May 27, 1936, 680–81.

————. "A Vein of Anthracite." *Brooklyn Daily Eagle*, December 20, 1936, 15C.

————. "Unanimity and Fortitude." *Poetry*, 49 (February 1937), 268–72.

————. "Statements." *Harvard Advocate*, 127 (December 1940), 31.

————. "There Is a War that Never Ends." *Kenyon Review*, 5 (Winter 1943), 144–47.

————. "The World Imagined . . . Since We Are Poor." *Poetry New York*, No. 4 (1951), 7–9.

————. "A Tribute." *Trinity Review*, 8 (May 1954), 11.

————. *Predilections*. New York: Viking Press, 1955.

————. *A Marianne Moore Reader*. New York: Viking Press, 1961.

————. "On Wallace Stevens." *New York Review of Books*, June 25, 1964, 5–6.

————. *The Complete Poems of Marianne Moore*. New York: Viking Press, 1981.

————. *The Complete Prose of Marianne Moore*. Ed. Patricia C. Willis. New York: Viking, Elizabeth Sifton Books, 1986.

Movius, Geoffrey. "'Two halves of . . . a fairly decent poet': William Carlos Williams and Ezra Pound 1914–1920." *The Visionary Company: A Magazine of the Twenties*, 1, No. 1 (Summer 1981), 121–48.

Nitchie, George. *Marianne Moore: An Introduction to the Poetry*. New York: Columbia University Press, 1969.

Ostriker, Alicia S. *Stealing the Language: The Emergence of Women's Poetry in America.* Boston: Beacon Press, 1986.

Parkes, H. B. "Two Pounds of Poetry." *New English Weekly,* (December 22, 1932), ii, 227–28. Rpt. in *Ezra Pound: The Critical Heritage,* ed. Eric Homberger. London and Boston: Routledge and Kegan Paul, 1972.

Pater, Walter. *The Renaissance.* 1910; rpt. Chicago: Academy Press, 1977.

Phelan, Margaret M. "H.D. and M.M.: Correspondences and Contradictions." Dissertation, Rutgers University, 1987.

Poirier, Richard. *A World Elsewhere: The Place of Style in American Literature.* New York: Oxford University Press, 1966.

Pound, Ezra. *Personae.* London: Elkin Mathews, 1909.

———. *Exultations.* London: Elkin Mathews, 1909.

———. *Canzoni.* London: Elkin Mathews, 1911.

———. "Drunken Helots and Mr. Eliot." *Egoist,* 4 (June 1917), 72–74.

———. *Lustra of Ezra Pound with Earlier Poems.* New York: For Private Circulation, October 1917.

———. *Pavannes and Divisions.* New York: Alfred A. Knopf, 1918.

———. "Marianne Moore and Mina Loy." *Little Review,* 10 (March 1918), 57–58.

———. "To the Editor of *The Athenaeum.*" *The Athenaeum,* October 31, 1919, 1132.

———. *Instigations.* New York: Boni and Liveright, 1920.

———. *Indiscretions.* Paris: Three Mountains Press, 1923.

———. *Antheil and the Treatise on Harmony.* Paris: Three Mountains Press, 1924.

———. *A Draft of XXX Cantos.* London: Faber and Faber, 1933.

———. *Literary Essays of Ezra Pound.* Ed. and intro. T. S. Eliot. New York: New Directions, 1968.

———. *The Selected Letters of Ezra Pound 1907–1941.* Ed. D. D. Paige. New York: New Directions Publishing Corp., 1971.

———. *ABC of Reading.* Norfolk, Ct.: New Directions Publishing Corp., n.d.

Sachs, Curt. *World History of the Dance.* Trans. Bessie Schönberg. New York: W. W. Norton and Company, 1937.

Saintsbury, George. *The Collected Essays and Papers of George Saintsbury 1875–1920.* Vol 2. London and Toronto: J. M. Dent & Sons, 1923.

Shulman, Grace. *Marianne Moore: The Poetry of Engagement.* Urbana and Chicago: University of Illinois Press, 1986.

Slatin, John. *The Savage's Romance: The Poetry of Marianne Moore*. University Park, Pa.: Pennsylvania State University Press, 1986.

Stapleton, Laurence. *Marianne Moore: The Poet's Advance*. Princeton: Princeton University Press, 1978.

Stevens, Wallace. *Harmonium*. New York: Alfred A. Knopf, 1923.

———. "A Poet that Matters." *Life and Letters Today*, 13 (December 1935), 61–65.

———. *Ideas of Order*. New York: Alcestis Press, 1935.

———. *Owl's Clover*. New York: Alcestis Press, 1936.

———. *The Man with the Blue Guitar and Other Poems*. New York: Alfred A. Knopf, 1937.

———. *Notes Toward a Supreme Fiction*. Mass.: Cummington Press, 1942.

———. *Transport to Summer*. New York: Alfred A. Knopf, 1947.

———. *The Auroras of Autumn*. New York: Alfred A. Knopf, 1950.

———. *The Necessary Angel: Essays on Reality and the Imagination*. New York: Vintage Books, 1951.

———. *Selected Poems*. London: Faber and Faber, 1953.

———. *Collected Poems of Wallace Stevens*. New York: Alfred A. Knopf, 1954.

———. *Opus Posthumous: Poems, Plays, Prose*. Ed. Samuel French Morse. 1957; rpt. New York: Vintage Books, 1982.

———. *The Palm at the End of the Mind: Selected Poems and a Play*. Ed. Holly Stevens. New York: Vintage Books, 1972.

———. Preface to *Collected Poems: 1921–1931*, by William Carlos Williams. New York: Objectivist Press, 1934. Rpt. in *William Carlos Williams: A Critical Anthology*, ed. Charles Tomlinson. Middlesex, England: Penguin Books, 1972.

———. *The Letters of Wallace Stevens*. Ed. Holly Stevens. New York: Alfred A. Knopf, 1977.

Sutton, Walter, ed. *Ezra Pound: A Collection of Critical Essays*. Englewood Cliffs, N. J.: Prentice-Hall, 1963.

Tate, Allen. "Ezra Pound's Golden Ass." *Nation*, June 10, 1931, 632–33.

Tomlinson, Charles, ed. *Marianne Moore: A Collection of Critical Essays*. Englewood Cliffs, N. J.: Prentice-Hall, 1969.

Vendler, Helen. *On Extended Wings: Wallace Stevens' Longer Poems*. Cambridge: Harvard University Press, 1969.

———. *Wallace Stevens: Words Chosen Out of Desire*. Cambridge: Harvard University Press, 1986.

Wasserstrom, William. *The Time of the Dial*. Syracuse: Syracuse University Press, 1963.

Weatherhead, A. Kingsley. *The Edge of the Image: Marianne Moore, William Carlos Williams and Some Other Poets*. Seattle and London: University of Washington Press, 1967.

Wescott, Glenway. "A Succession of Poets." *Partisan Review*, 50, No. 3 (1983), 392–406.

Wilde, Oscar. *The Artist as Critic: Critical Writings of Oscar Wilde*. Ed. Richard Ellman. New York: Random House, 1968.

Willard, Abbie F. *Wallace Stevens: The Poet and His Critics*. Chicago: American Library Association, 1978.

Williams, William Carlos. *Kora in Hell: Improvisations*. Boston: Four Seas Company, 1920.

———. *The Great American Novel*. Paris: Three Mountains Press, 1923.

———. *In the American Grain*. New York: Albert and Charles Boni, 1925.

———. "Marianne Moore." *The Dial*, 78 (May 1925), 393–401.

———. *Collected Poems: 1921–1931*. New York: Objectivist Press, 1934.

———. *An Early Martyr and Other Poems*. New York: Alcestis Press, 1935.

———. "Excerpts from a Critical Sketch: *A Draft of XXX Cantos* by Ezra Pound." In *Selected Essays of William Carlos Williams*. New York: Random House, 1954. Rpt. in *Ezra Pound: A Collection of Critical Essays*. Englewood Cliffs, N.J.: Prentice-Hall, 1963.

———. *I Wanted to Write a Poem: The Autobiography of the Works of a Poet*. Ed. Edith Heal. 1958; rpt. New York: New Directions Publishing Corp., 1978.

———. *Paterson*. New York: New Directions Publishing Corp., 1963.

Willis, Patricia C. "Marianne Moore and Peter Morris: Facts and Speculations." *Marianne Moore Newsletter*, 1, No. 1 (Spring 1977), 14–15.

———. "Marianne Moore on Ezra Pound 1901–1915." *Marianne Moore Newsletter*, 3 (Fall 1979), 5–8.

Wimsatt, William K., and Cleanth Brooks. *Literary Criticism: A Short History*. 2 vols. Chicago and London: University of Chicago Press, 1957.

Yeats, W. B. Introduction to *The Oxford Book of Modern Verse*, ed. W. B. Yeats. London: Oxford University Press, 1936. Rpt. in *Ezra Pound: A Collection of Critical Essays*, ed. Walter Sutton. Englewood Cliffs, N.J.: Prentice-Hall, 1963.

Index